# Advocacy
*and*
## Educational Technology

A Guide to Getting Your Voice Heard

*Hilary Goldmann*

*Hilary Goldman*
*Keep advocating!*

International Society for Technology in Education
EUGENE, OREGON • WASHINGTON, DC

# Advocacy *and* Educational Technology
## A Guide to Getting Your Voice Heard

*Hilary Goldmann*

Director of Book Publishing: *Courtney Burkholder*
Acquisitions Editor: *Jeff V. Bolkan*
Production Editors: *Tina Wells, Lynda Gansel*
Production Coordinator: *Rachel Williams*
Graphic Designer: *Signe Landin*
Developmental Editor: *Sharleen Nelson*
Copy Editor: *Kathy Hamman*
Proofreader: *Katherine Gries*
Cover Design, Book Design, and Production: *Signe Landin*

### Library of Congress Cataloging-in-Publication Data

Goldmann, Hilary.
   Advocacy and educational technology : a guide to getting your voice heard / Hilary Goldmann. — 1st ed.
      p. cm.
   Includes bibliographical references.
   ISBN 978-1-56484-310-4 (pbk.)
1. Educational technology.     I. Title.
   LB1028.3.G64 2011
   371.33—dc23

                                                        2011039118

First Edition
ISBN: 978-1-56484-310-4
Printed in the United States of America

*Cover & Title Page Image:* ©iStockphoto.com/Andreas Rodriguez
*Inside Images:* pg. 3: ©iStockphoto.com/claudiobaba, pg. 17: ©iStockphoto.com/Dwight Nadig, pg. 25: ©iStockphoto.com/Steve Debenport, pg. 37: ©iStockphoto.com/Leontura, pg. 49: ©iStockphoto.com/Chris Schmidt, pg. 61: ©iStockphoto.com/Robert Churchill

ISTE® is a registered trademark of the International Society for Technology in Education.

# About ISTE

The International Society for Technology in Education (ISTE) is the trusted source for professional development, knowledge generation, advocacy, and leadership for innovation. ISTE is the premier membership association for educators and education leaders engaged in improving teaching and learning by advancing the effective use of technology in PK–12 and teacher education.

Home of the National Educational Technology Standards (NETS) and ISTE's annual conference and exposition (formerly known as NECC), ISTE represents more than 100,000 professionals worldwide. We support our members with information, networking opportunities, and guidance as they face the challenge of transforming education. To find out more about these and other ISTE initiatives, visit our website at www.iste.org.

As part of our mission, ISTE Book Publishing works with experienced educators to develop and produce practical resources for classroom teachers, teacher educators, and technology leaders. Every manuscript we select for publication is carefully peer-reviewed and professionally edited. We value your feedback on this book and other ISTE products. E-mail us at books@iste.org.


**International Society for Technology in Education**
Washington, DC, Office:
   1710 Rhode Island Ave. NW, Suite 900, Washington, DC 20036-3132
Eugene, Oregon, Office:
   180 West 8th Ave., Suite 300, Eugene, OR 97401-2916
Order Desk: 1.800.336.5191
Order Fax: 1.541.302.3778
Customer Service: orders@iste.org
Book Publishing: books@iste.org
Book Sales and Marketing: booksmarketing@iste.org
Web: www.iste.org

# About the Author

Senior Director of Government Affairs for the International Society for Technology in Education (ISTE), Hilary Goldmann has more than 20 years of experience working in the public policy and advocacy arenas. She is responsible for developing and executing ISTE's federal and state public policy agendas and mobilizing its grassroots efforts. Her "Voices Carry" column is a regular feature of ISTE's *Learning & Leading with Technology* magazine, and her "inside the beltway" presentations are popular features at ISTE Affiliates' state conferences and other national conferences. Goldmann is a recognized leader and partner in the education association and corporate community.

Before joining ISTE in July 2005, she led the Higher Education Information Technology (HEIT) Alliance, a coalition of 10 U.S. higher education and library associations established to promote the higher education and library communities' interests in federal information technology policy. Prior to her work with the HEIT Alliance, she was the director of congressional relations at the American Association of State Colleges and Universities (AASCU), where she headed up AASCU's policy and advocacy efforts on budget and appropriations, teacher preparation, information technology, science education and research, and managed the association's grassroots activities.

Goldmann began working in public policy as an aide to former U.S. Senator Howard Metzenbaum. She is a graduate of the State University of New York at Binghamton.

## Acknowledgments

I would like to acknowledge ISTE's Board of Directors for their leadership in recognizing the importance of advocacy for a global membership organization, and the ISTE Public Policy and Advocacy Committee for its guidance in developing ISTE's advocacy agenda. I am especially grateful to ISTE's committed members for embracing the call to advocacy.

# Contents

Contents

# Preface

ISTE members often approach me to say that they are interested in getting involved in advocacy but don't know how to get started. Many seem hesitant to become involved because they are unsure if policy makers are interested in what they have to say. It is important that you make your voice heard, and policy makers do listen to constituents. How will a policy maker know that classroom technology is important unless you tell them? In response to the growing importance and interest in advocacy, ISTE established the Voices Carry advocacy campaign to help ISTE members strengthen their voices to effect change at all levels of government. This booklet, *Advocacy and Educational Technology: A Guide to Getting Your Voice Heard*, is one component of the Voices Carry campaign.

Most of the references in this book have to do with policies and programs in the United States. However, there is much to be gleaned by readers in any country. We encourage you to apply the principles and examples given to the environments in your local, regional, and national government structures.

## How Much Time Do You Have?

*Advocacy and Educational Technology* is designed to share some of the most pressing policy issues for education technology advocates as well as to provide you with the tools and resources to get started. In fact, here are four ways to get started advocating today, based on how much time you have:

- **Two minutes?** Spread the word. Send a pre-composed letter or email through the Ed Tech Action Network (ETAN) at www.edtechactionnetwork.org and share this website with five friends.

- **Five minutes?** Develop an effective "elevator" speech. Imagine yourself in a situation where you unexpectedly come into contact with someone who could be instrumental in raising support for educational technology. You have less than a minute to make a positive impression on this person.

- **Fifteen minutes?** Educate yourself and join the conversation. Hear it from the source: Hilary Goldmann, ISTE's senior director of government affairs, shares the latest advocacy news from Washington, D.C., as it happens (www.iste-community.org/profiles/blog/list?user=HilaryGoldmann).

- **Sixty minutes or more?** Set up a meeting with a policy maker or the person's staff. Can't get to D.C.? That's okay. Policy makers have offices throughout their states, and members of Congress or their staff members will meet with you. This is a great way to share your expertise and become the go-to person for advice to share with fellow advocates.

Each of us has the responsibility to seize opportunities to influence federal, state, and local policies. We need to band together and make our voices heard!

The purpose of this guide is twofold: to help you better understand the ongoing issues we face and to provide the references and tools to help you become involved in making a difference.

## Chapter 1

# What Is Advocacy?

*Never doubt that a small group of thoughtful, committed citizens can change the world. Indeed, it's the only thing that ever has.*

*—Margaret Mead*

The International Society for Technology in Education (ISTE®) is the premier membership association for educators and education leaders engaged in improving learning and teaching by advancing the effective use of technology in PK–12 and teacher education. ISTE represents more than 100,000 education leaders and emerging leaders throughout the world and informs its members regarding educational issues of national and global scope.

ISTE members include individuals, affiliate organizations, and corporations:

- 20,000+ individual members
- 80 affiliate organizations
- 89 individual member countries
- 6 affiliate regions worldwide
- 65 corporations worldwide

ISTE membership is a powerful and meaningful way for educators to connect with peers, to gather in a variety of forums to share the challenges and excitement of teaching, and to be part of a community that leads the transformation of education.

## Advocacy—A Top Priority for ISTE and the Author

In 2002, ISTE opened an office in Washington, D.C., to help advance one of its top priorities: advocacy of technology in education at the federal level in the United States. As ISTE's senior director of government affairs, I am responsible for raising ISTE's visibility and influence inside the beltway and for growing ISTE's grassroots efforts, spending a great deal of time directing policy meetings and working in concert with other organizations and business groups to develop and advance a united educational technology message.

With ISTE's support and in cooperation with other organizations, I have worked on updating provisions of the Enhancing Education Through Technology program (EETT), revising it as the Achievement Through Technology and Innovation Act (ATTAIN), which was introduced in the Senate by a bipartisan committee in April 2009, and, since that time, advocated for passage of ATTAIN, either as part of the Elementary and Secondary Education Act (ESEA) reauthorization or as a stand-alone measure.

"Inside the beltway" refers to the U.S. political system, much of which resides within the Capital Beltway (U.S. Interstate 495).

EETT is also known as *E2T2*.

ESEA is spelled out: *E-S-E-A*.

In April 2011, the Enhancing Education Through Technology program was completely cut by Congress, a disappointing action because EETT was the only federal funding stream that was allocated exclusively to developing better educational technology. However, this was expected because it had been eliminated from President Obama's proposed budget. Instead of having EETT or a successor program as a separate, directed federal program, the administration proposes to infuse technology throughout the 11 major funding priorities that the Obama administration supports in a refashioned ESEA.

(For more details, see www.iste-community.org/profiles/blogs/ed-tech-eliminated-in-final, my blog post from April 12, 2011: "Ed Tech Eliminated in Final Budget Bill for FY 11.")

# Defining Advocacy

In simplest terms, *Merriam-Webster Online Dictionary* (2011) defines advocacy as "the act or process of advocating or supporting a cause or proposal." Yet, advocacy is even more than that. It's caring deeply enough about an issue to stand up and demand that your voice be heard by the people who have the power to make the changes.

# Why Is Advocacy Important?

Advocacy for congressional support of technology in education is absolutely vital to the future of our children. This is our central message. Federal policy makers in Washington D.C. are facing increased pressures to tighten budgets, and even when they hear from constituents, as we have seen in 2011, they are capable of cutting funds from key programs—including those that keep classrooms competitive through education technology. Without a vocal constituency advocating for funding—as well as restoration of much-needed funds—in their home districts, elected officials can all too easily ignore the needs of 21st-century learners.

Each member of Congress relies on staff members, who in turn handle a large portfolio of policy issues. For instance, the staff person who handles education (this would include PK–higher education) may also handle healthcare, agriculture, housing, and labor issues. So, when meeting with this staff person and sharing information about education technology, it is important to note that five minutes later there will be someone else in the office meeting with this same staff person, and that someone will share vital information about a completely different policy area.

Even if I make a compelling presentation, how can we ensure that the message will resonate and land high on the list of priorities for this member of Congress? The best way to make sure my message is heard is by reminding this and every member of Congress that my voice represents those of numerous constituents.

Constituents' voices are those that really resound in the halls of Congress. Members of Congress must hear from the people who vote for them, or else they will not know that education technology issues (among other issues) are a priority for their district. The grassroots component of influencing funding decisions is critical. Policy makers have many competing demands weighing on them; therefore, it is the education technology community's responsibility to make sure they hear our message. This is the way an issue gets on the priority list—complementary and multiple messages resonating from the districts. Every victory is a celebration, but advocacy is ongoing.

## What Is Lobbying?

Lobbying is a form of advocacy with the goal of influencing decisions made by legislators and other officials in the government. ISTE is a 501(c)(3) organization. We are allowed to lobby, but we are restricted from political campaigning. Put another way, ISTE may take sides with respect to political issues, but not political candidates. Additionally, we have elected to follow the 501(h) lobbying expenditure test, which provides strict financial limits for our lobbying expenditures.

Lobbying can be either *direct* or *grassroots*. Direct lobbying involves contacting legislators or their staffs about specific legislation and providing a view on the legislation. Grassroots lobbying attempts to influence legislation through communications with the general public. The public is urged to contact their legislators in support of or in opposition to legislation. My representation of ISTE's membership includes both direct and grassroots work.

### Direct Lobbying

An example of direct lobbying is when I meet with policy makers and ask them to take a specific position with regard to a policy issue. Often I meet with Congressional staff and encourage their boss to sponsor or co-sponsor a particular piece of legislation, vote a particular way on a piece of legislation, or provide a certain amount of funding for a particular federal program.

### *Grassroots Lobbying*

Grassroots lobbying occurs when I reach out to ISTE members and inform them about policy issues and encourage them to take action. ISTE does this in various ways, ranging from communicating via the Education Technology Action Network, sending email messages to various ISTE communication channels such as the ISTE affiliates and the SIGs (special interest groups), and ISTE advocacy professional development activities. ISTE's grassroots lobbying activities are focused on increasing the number of education technology advocates and supporting these individuals in their advocacy endeavors.

As part of our grassroots lobbying activities, ISTE is leveraging social media tools such as ISTE Connects, ISTE Ning, ISTE's Facebook page, and Twitter. We are investigating new ways to leverage social media for advocacy and have held a "Tweet for Ed Tech" day.

## Successful Lobbying

Through ISTE's Board of Directors and Public Policy and Advocacy Committee, we develop a U.S. Public Policy Principles and Federal and State Objectives document to guide our policy activities for the year. This document states: "ISTE's public policy principles and federal and state objectives are founded upon our members' uncompromising commitment to provide students the technology and information skills and tools necessary for success in the 21st century."

Coalitions—such as the Committee for Education Funding (www.cef.org), America's largest education coalition that reflects a broad spectrum of the education community (PK–20); the Education and Library Networks Coalition (www.edlinc.org), focusing on the E-Rate program; and the National Coalition for Technology in Education and Training (www.nctet.org)— are indispensable for gaining allies and working in concert to achieve our policy goals and to bring ISTE's message to a broad range of education, corporate, and public service organizations.

The key to lobbying effectively is knowing how to integrate activities, depending on the issue at hand, to achieve success. I am able to tap the ISTE membership's expertise through formal and informal channels to garner advice, guidance, and timely feedback when developing legislative proposals and monitoring legislation that is moving in the halls of Congress. ISTE members have served as crucial resources in helping to guide our policy positions on No Child Left Behind (NCLB/ESEA), E-Rate, EETT, ATTAIN, and teacher preparation legislation.

# ISTE's Advocacy Role

As a diverse, worldwide community of educational leaders who actively create learning environments in which all students can achieve their creative and intellectual potential, ISTE is globally recognized as the premier partner in advancing educational excellence through innovative learning, teaching, and leadership. ISTE, whose mission is to "advance excellence in learning and teaching through innovative and effective uses of technology," also acknowledges that without proper funding, educators will not have the tools and means to bring technology to the classroom. Effective advocacy is critical in advancing the field and achieving the mission and vision of the organization. Thus, by championing innovation, access, and global stewardship in all its advocacy and educational activities, ISTE is dedicated to bringing the voice of educators to policy makers in terms of educational technology.

Advocacy is most effective when combined with action. Although it is important to state goals and objectives clearly, it is equally important to back up a position with concrete actions to achieve those goals and objectives. ISTE's advocacy initiatives bring "the voice of local educators to the nation's policy makers." At the same time, ISTE is developing advocacy expertise among educators so that they can be valuable informational resources for policy makers at all levels of government.

How does ISTE go about actually influencing federal policy and debate? ISTE achieves its policy goals through a combination of the following:

- public policy development and analysis
- direct lobbying
- coalition building
- grassroots mobilization
- media outreach

In addition to the ISTE affiliate network, ISTE special interest groups (SIGs) are stepping up their advocacy game. The Teacher Educators Special Interest Group (SIGTE) took the lead in developing the Preparing Teachers for Digital Age Learners program, and both the Administrators SIG (SIGAdmin) and the SIG Media Specialists have developed advocacy platforms.

# ISTE's U.S. Public Policy Principles and Federal and State Objectives

ISTE's public policy principles and federal and state objectives are founded upon its members' uncompromising commitment to provide students the technology and information skills and tools necessary for success in the 21st century. ISTE strongly believes that the effective use of technology can drive academic success and help prepare all learners for post-secondary education, careers, and life. Proper integration of modern digital tools and content into the learning environment by trained administrators and teachers will lead to high-achieving citizens equipped to succeed in our evolving global society.

ISTE's public policy objectives are based on the following seven core principles:

1. Technology is an essential element of teaching, learning, and instructional design in effective, engaging, 21st-century learning systems.

2. Fluency with technology must be embedded in the learning process and is a prerequisite for attaining necessary 21st-century skills to ensure academic success and workforce preparedness.

3. Preservice and sustained inservice professional development of teachers and administrators must include instruction on integrating technology into the learning process.

4. The success of student achievement is affected by data collection, which includes best practices regarding data collection for schools. Analysis of data provides for real-time intervention that is enhanced through technology.

5. Sustained research and development at the national level is essential to drive innovation in teaching and learning in educational environments.

6. Application of high-quality, research-based findings and best practices in educational technology must become part of the education system.

7. Students must have robust Internet and network access no matter where they live and no matter what their socioeconomic circumstances.

## Leadership—White House and Department of Education

ISTE believes that leadership for using technology effectively for teaching and learning must start at the White House and with the Office of the Secretary of Education. A strong commitment and focus that ensures teachers are proficient in imparting the skills necessary for the digital age and harnessing modern digital tools and content for classroom learning is critical. ISTE will advocate for a school innovation focus at the highest levels of the White House and Department of Education as well as for strengthening the Office of Educational Technology at the Department of Education.

## Budget and Appropriations

ISTE will take a lead role in building support for increasing annual appropriations for federal education technology programs. Specifically, ISTE will be at the forefront in advocating for restoring funding for the Enhancing Education Through Technology program (EETT), which is Title II-D of the Elementary and Secondary Education Act (ESEA), also known as the No Child Left Behind (NCLB) Act; the Preparing Teachers for Digital Age Learners (PTDAL) program; and subsequent programs in the next iterations of the ESEA.

Together these programs can provide a significant boost to ensure that our nation's schools are equipped with the latest technology tools and content, and that current and new teachers have the skills and know-how to use these tools and content effectively for improved classroom teaching and learning.

## Cyber Safety and Security

Keeping our students safe online, teaching them to use digital tools and content in an ethical and responsible manner, and ensuring that our school networks are secure are basic tenets of school and district professionals. ISTE will continue to support efforts that educate students on how to stay safe online and will promote secure school networks.

## Elementary and Secondary Education Act (ESEA) Reauthorization

The next iteration of our nation's K–12 law, the Elementary and Secondary Education Act (ESEA), must help transform U.S. elementary and secondary schools into modern, technology-rich, digital learning environments. Revamping the Enhancing

Education Through Technology program (EETT) as the Achievement Through Technology and Innovation Act (ATTAIN) and strengthening and adding technology components to other provisions of the legislation will ensure students succeed in the 21st century both academically and in the workplace. More specifically, ISTE is leading efforts to accomplish the following:

1. Pass the Achievement Through Technology and Innovation Act (ATTAIN) as part of the Elementary and Secondary Education Act (ESEA) reauthorization or as a stand-alone measure. The ATTAIN Act would update and replace the Enhancing Education Through Technology (EETT) program by building on its successes and focusing resources on those practices known to best leverage technology for educational improvement. The ATTAIN Act (S. 818 and H.R. 558) was introduced in the Senate by a bipartisan group on April 2, 2009.

2. Use data to affect student learning at the classroom level. Funding should be allocated to districts to build capacity for data systems to benchmark and chart student progress throughout the school year. These data systems will provide teachers and administrators with the necessary data components that would allow schools to assess, interpret, and implement appropriate interventions that provide each student a path to meet state standards and pass state-mandated exams and proficiencies. The data program, including key components of professional development for teachers and administrators, would help schools and districts implement a plan for continuous school improvement.

3. Ensure that our nation's educators are proficient in effectively integrating technology into the learning environment. Current educators should demonstrate with performance-based evidence the ability to use modern information tools and digital content to support student learning in content areas and for assessment and learning management. Future teachers should successfully complete instructional technology coursework that achieves this goal.

## Intellectual Property

Educators and students currently adhere to the Copyright and Fair Use Guidelines for use of copyrighted material to support the instructional process and will continue to do so as material moves from print to digital format. The debate between owners and users of copyrighted materials continued during the 111th Congress, from January 3, 2009, through January 3, 2011. ISTE monitored these activities and partnered as appropriate with various stakeholders.

## Research and Development (R&D) for Innovation in Teaching and Learning

Targeting federal resources toward research and development for innovation in teaching and learning is critical if the United States is to continue to be a global leader in education. ISTE will support federal leadership in R&D as well as dissemination and application of these research findings throughout the education system.

## Science, Technology, Engineering, and Mathematics (STEM)

The nature of science, technology, engineering, and mathematics (STEM) careers has changed—today's scientists, information technologists, mathematicians, and engineers spend a significant portion of their time using simulations and other technology tools to achieve their goals. STEM curriculum in our nation's schools must evolve and be aligned with the modern methods that today's STEM professionals use in their daily work. ISTE will advocate for federal initiatives that focus on STEM— from graduating more students in STEM disciplines to funding STEM curriculum in K–12 schools. Federal initiatives must include provisions to ensure that the use and implementation of modern digital tools and content are an integral part of these activities.

Within the Obama administration's blueprint for revising the ESEA, see www2.ed. gov/policy/elsec/leg/blueprint/faq/supporting-stem.pdf for the section titled "Supporting Science, Technology, Engineering, and Mathematics Education."

## Telecommunications Broadband Connectivity

### *Broadband Connectivity*

Schools and school districts are becoming increasingly dependent on the Internet for teaching and learning as well as administrative tasks. Unfortunately, many schools' networks do not have the capacity to meet the needs of these increased demands. ISTE will continue to advocate for federal telecommunications policy that will assist schools in upgrading their networks to meet the growing demand of today's applications and systems.

### *E-Rate*

The Universal Service Schools and Libraries (E-Rate) program is a U.S. government program, created as part of the Telecommunications Act of 1996, that enables schools and libraries to purchase telecommunications and Internet service at a discounted rate. The E-Rate program has had the most direct impact of any education technology program on our nation's schools and continues to be a critical investment in ensuring that schools have the financial resources to connect to the Internet. School funding needs, however, outstrip available E-Rate funding by $1 billion each year. ISTE has led efforts to raise the funding cap for the E-Rate program. The Federal Communications Commission issued an order on September 23, 2010, to upgrade E-Rate, which is tied to the rate of inflation. (See www.fcc.gov/Daily_Releases/Daily_Business/2010/db1001/FCC-10-175A1.pdf for information from the FCC on its September 2010 order.) Additional detailed information on E-Rate is included in Chapters 2 and 5.

## Workforce Development

Technology is an integral part of almost every job or profession today. The preparation of our students for their careers, referred to as Career Technical Education or Workforce Development, is being recognized as an essential national priority. ISTE, working with other partners, supports efforts that prepare our nation's students to succeed in careers for today's global economy.

## ISTE's Federal and State Government Strategies and Grassroots Mobilization

In working to achieve these policy objectives, ISTE will, as appropriate, collaborate with other organizations and coalitions, rely on the ISTE affiliate network, and call on the Education Technology Action Network (ETAN, known as the Ed Tech Action Network, www.edtechactionnetwork.org) at critical times to ensure that the administration and members of Congress hear from ISTE members.

ISTE encourages all 50 states, the District of Columbia, and U.S. Territories to join with it to provide leadership to improve teaching and learning by advancing the effective use of technology in education. ISTE believes federal lawmakers, governors, and state legislators should embrace legislation and other policy initiatives to harness technology to meet federal and individual state education goals, accomplish the student achievement objectives of the Elementary and Secondary Education Act (ESEA), and empower teachers, administrators, and students toward greater innovation.

ETAN rhymes with *began.*

Through ISTE's affiliate organizations and ETAN, ISTE will strengthen our grassroots ability to influence policy at the federal and state level. ISTE will be a catalyst and resource for affiliate organizations to increase their involvement in the advocacy and policy arena. Through professional development opportunities, information sharing, and the power of ETAN, ISTE can help individual state organizations identify, articulate, implement, and realize their state policy objectives.

Affiliate organizations can take several avenues to influence change at the state level:

- They should evaluate existing state education programs to determine the opportunities for making changes to these programs that will help to modernize schools and graduate 21st-century learners.

- They may choose to analyze the political climate in their states to determine if opportunities exist to create programs that will direct additional state funds for education technology.

- They may choose to identify opportunities for new education technology activities within their states that focus on the following categories: student achievement and 21st-century skills, teacher and administrator professional development, curriculum and materials development, and infrastructure and access.

# Federal-Level Policies Impact Classroom Learning

Now that we have identified the strategies meant to impact policy at the federal level, we need to ask the question: Do decisions made by policy makers at the federal level really have a direct impact on classroom learning? It is true that education policy and funding historically have been and continue to be primarily a local/state responsibility. In fact, less than 12 percent of U.S. education funding comes directly from the federal government. The U.S. Department of Education's website contains the following information (March 30, 2011) that many citizens may find surprising:

> Of an estimated $1.13 trillion being spent nationwide on education at all levels for school year 2010–2011, a substantial majority will come from state, local, and private sources. This is especially true at the elementary and secondary level, where about 89.2 percent of the funds will come from non-Federal sources.

That means the Federal contribution to elementary and secondary education is about 10.8 percent, which includes funds not only from the Department of Education (ED) but also from other Federal agencies, such as the Department of Health and Human Services' Head Start program and the Department of Agriculture's School Lunch program. (www2.ed.gov/about/overview/fed/role.html)

This federal money, however, comes with strings attached—certain requirements, assessments, and accountability measures that must be adhered to in exchange for receiving these monies. Most school districts accept these dollars with their requirements rather than forego the funds, thus providing the federal government with significant influence and direction setting for the nation's education agenda.

Since the NCLB Act became the law of the land in 2002, we have witnessed how decisions made inside the beltway do indeed have a direct impact on local decision making and, consequently, on the teaching and learning taking place in our nation's classrooms through mandates such as standardized testing and requirements for adequate yearly progress. More specifically, the impact of federal policy on the infusion of digital tools and content in the classroom and in teacher preparation programs can be illustrated by the E-Rate program; the Enhancing Education Through Technology (EETT; E2T2) program, which was Title II-Part D of the NCLB Act of 2001; and the Preparing Tomorrow's Teachers to Use Technology (PT$^3$) program. The PT$^3$ program of 1998 was replaced by its successor, the Preparing Teachers for Digital Age Learners (PTDAL) program in 2006.

Because advocacy is an important activity to bring about change in public attitudes and policies that impact education, here are 10 reasons why all of us who care about our children's futures need to participate in advocacy:

1. You can make a difference.

2. People working together can make a difference.

3. People can change laws.

4. Lobbying is a democratic tradition.

5. Advocacy and lobbying help find real solutions.

6. Advocacy (and lobbying) is easy and fun (once you understand the rules and know what works).

7. Policy makers need your expertise.

8. Advocacy and lobbying can help people.

9. The views of local organizations are important.

10. Advocacy and lobbying advance your cause and build public trust.

Those of us with a passion and commitment for improving teaching and learning by advancing the effective use of technology to transform our nation's schools, increasing student achievement, and ensuring that our students develop the skills they need to succeed in the 21st century must band together and make our voices heard!

# Chapter 2

# A Brief History of U.S. Programs and Policy Issues

The Elementary and Secondary Act of 1965 (ESEA) was one of many antipoverty initiatives developed under President Lyndon Johnson's Great Society programs of the 1960s. Title I was enacted to help schools in communities with high concentrations of poor children.

# Enhancing Education Through Technology (EETT)

The No Child Left Behind (NCLB) legislation that was proposed by President George W. Bush in 2001 included a new education technology program called the Enhancing Education Through Technology program (EETT). Under EETT, the U.S. Secretary of Education allocates funds directly to states based on the number of disadvantaged students eligible for federal assistance. After reserving 5 percent for state activities, the states in turn allocate 50 percent of this funding to local education agencies (LEAs), based on the number of disadvantaged students

NCLB is pronounced *nickel-bee.*

in the LEA. The rest of the funding is awarded to LEAs through a competitive grant program administered at the state level. The EETT was designed to undergird NCLB's goals by supporting professional development; the implementation of educational software and digital content for use in the areas of curriculum, instruction, and classroom/school administration; computer-assisted and online testing; data-driven decision-making systems; and technology-based strategies to improve parental involvement. It also includes the goal that all students be technologically literate by the eighth grade.

# Authorization vs. Reauthorization

Authorization is what creates the law, program, or agency. In 2002, after Congress passed NCLB, the president signed the NCLB authorization, which was a reauthorization of the 1965 ESEA. The NCLB authorization took the programs that were already in existence, such as Title I that provided funding to schools with disadvantaged kids, and made changes to those provisions. No Child Left Behind made changes to an existing program and created something brand new. The NCLB law had an expiration date of September 30, 2007, but Congress has continued to pass legislation to keep its provisions in place and to fund its programs.

Comprehensive legislation like ESEA creates programs such as Title I and the Enhancing Education Through Technology program. The ESEA law includes language that "authorizes" funding for these programs. The appropriations process determines how much funding the various programs will actually receive. The authorization level—the amount of funding the law says the government can provide—is often greater than the actual appropriated level. Additionally, the government authorizes programs for a finite period, requiring Congress to review the programs on a regular basis and make changes to them or to eliminate programs that are no longer relevant. We call this review and modification process reauthorization, and this is what we are continuing to work on for ESEA.

> The Obama administration's blueprint to overhaul the No Child Left Behind Act (NCLB) will support state and local efforts to help ensure that all students graduate prepared for college and a career.

> Following the lead of the nation's governors and state education leaders, the plan will ask states to ensure that their academic standards prepare students to succeed in college and the workplace, and to create accountability systems that recognize student growth and school progress toward meeting that goal. This will be a key priority in the reform of NCLB, which was signed into law in 2002 and is the most recent reauthorization of the Elementary and Secondary Education Act of 1965 (ESEA).

> "We will work with Congress on a bipartisan basis to reauthorize ESEA this year," Secretary of Education Arne Duncan said about the blueprint, which the Obama administration released on [March 13, 2010]. (www2.ed.gov/policy/elsec/leg/blueprint/; see "released" link)

# The American Recovery and Reinvestment Act (ARRA)

The American Recovery and Reinvestment Act (ARRA), signed into law by President Obama on February 17, 2009, directed more than $100 billion to education. This is the largest one-time federal infusion of funds for education ever. ISTE worked closely with the Obama administration and the U.S. Congress to ensure that the ARRA included a dedicated funding stream for classroom technology and professional development through the Enhancing Education Through Technology program (EETT, Title II, Part D of NCLB). In addition to the EETT program funds, ARRA also included opportunities to invest in classroom technology, Title I, and Individuals with Disabilities Education Act (IDEA).

# Achievement Through Technology and Innovation Act (ATTAIN)

Some members of Congress have introduced individual bills that they hope will later be included in the final reauthorization of ESEA. One of these bills is the Achievement Through Technology and Innovation Act (ATTAIN). The ATTAIN Act would update and replace the EETT program by building on its successes and focusing resources on those practices known to best leverage technology for educational improvement. This act focuses on systemic redesign, innovation, and professional development for both administrators and teachers. It also strengthens the existing eighth grade technology literacy component. The ATTAIN Act recognizes learning technologies as critical for our schools—to meet No Child Left Behind's goals of raising student achievement and ensuring high quality teaching, and to ensure that our nation's students are prepared to compete in the 21st century.

# E-Rate

The Universal Service Administrative Company's Schools and Libraries "E-Rate" program has had the most direct impact of any education technology program on our nation's schools. Listening to their constituents in the education and library communities, Congress recognized the growing importance of new technologies and the Internet for improving education via student access to critical information. The E-Rate program was created as part of the Telecommunications Act of 1996, under the auspices of the Federal Communications Commission (FCC). It provides $2.25 billion annually in discounts to schools and libraries for telecommunications services, Internet access, and internal connections, yet annual demands on the fund routinely exceed the program's $2.25 billion cap.

The E-Rate program provides discounts to public and private schools, public libraries, and consortia of those entities. The discounts apply to telecommunications services, Internet access, and internal networking. E-Rate discounts are provided through the FCC by assessing telecommunication carriers to offset the cost of the discounts. This methodology follows a long-established Universal Service Fund model, which has been used to ensure affordable access to telephone services for residents in all areas of the nation for more than 65 years. E-Rate discounts range from 20 to 90 percent, based on local poverty levels. Schools and libraries must pay the undiscounted portion of their telecommunications bills themselves. Discounts are determined by the percentage of students eligible for the national school lunch program and by the school (or consortium's) urban/rural designation.

The resounding success of this program is evident in the following comparison: In 1996, 14 percent of our nation's classrooms were connected to the Internet; today more than 94 percent of them are connected. The federal E-Rate program was the catalyst for this significant achievement.

Without the E-Rate program, the Internet connection in many of our nation's classrooms, particularly those in under-resourced neighborhoods, simply would not exist. Although most of the nation's classrooms are connected to the Internet, the job of the E-Rate program is not complete. Connectivity is no longer enough if the speed is inadequate for today's technology applications. Schools rely on the E-Rate program to upgrade their connectivity and expand their bandwidth capabilities to keep up with current and future demands on their networks. ISTE is on record as recommending to the FCC that schools be supported as they strive for adequate bandwidth and speed for the following connections in the next several years:

- connection speeds within and between wide-area networks (WANs)

- connection speeds between WANs and district buildings

- connection speeds inside the building to the desktop computing device or wireless router

Maintaining optimal services means that students, teachers, and community members will continue to enjoy access without delay to valuable online materials and resources, such as electronic card catalogs and grade books; interactive whiteboards for classroom lessons; video-streamed content to augment in-classroom lessons; videoconferencing equipment to communicate with schools around the country and across the globe; and collaborative learning technologies, such as interactive educational simulations.

Over the last several years there have been congressional efforts to eliminate the E-Rate program, and an accounting change was made that forced the program to shut down for several months in 2004. Clearly, it is essential to keep members of Congress apprised of the E-Rate program's benefits to schools and communities, ensuring their continued support for it.

# Preparing Teachers for Digital Age Learners (PTDAL)

Established by the Clinton administration and enacted into law as part of the Higher Education Act reauthorization in 1998, the then-named Preparing Tomorrow's Teachers to Use Technology (PT³) program was created to prepare prospective teachers to use advanced technology to help all students meet challenging state and local academic achievement standards and to improve the ability of institutions of higher education to carry out such training. This federal grant program provided funds to institutions of higher education and other teacher education programs to prepare new teachers to use technology in the classroom.

When a federal administration leaves office, it is not unusual for its priority programs to lose their priority with the succeeding administration, and this is what happened to the PT³ program when the Bush administration took office. With no leadership from the White House to support PT³, no member of Congress to champion the program, and a lack of a vocal grassroots constituency, the funding for PT³ languished until the program was completely eliminated.

In 2006 Congress passed a reauthorization of the Higher Education Act. In a major victory for education technology supporters, the legislation included a new program—Preparing Teachers for Digital Age Learners (PTDAL)—a successor to the PT³ program. PTDAL awards grants to consortia led by higher education institutions to assure that graduating "teacher candidates … are prepared to use modern information, communication, and learning tools." Grants are for no more than $2 million and last for three years, with an optional one-year renewal. The law mandates a 25 percent matching requirement by the participating consortia. Specifically, PTDAL provides consortia with two options to address the preparation of our nation's teachers:

■ developing long-term partnerships focused on effective teaching with modern digital tools and content that substantially connect preservice preparation of teacher candidates with high-needs schools

■ transforming the way schools of education teach classroom technology integration to teacher candidates

Awards made under the PTDAL program support systemic initiatives aligned with local technology plans and with state teacher and student technology standards.

# Funding

With a $1 billion authorization, EETT could have significantly transitioned our schools into 21st-century learning environments. However, an authorization does not automatically turn into funding. "Authorizing legislation," such as NCLB, is legislation that creates programs and provides guidelines as to how much funding can potentially be spent on individual programs. The authorizing legislation, however, does not fund the programs. Another legislative track called the "appropriations process" actually funds the programs. The appropriations or funding decisions are made annually, which means each year Congress determines, for example, how much funding each program under NCLB will receive.

To make things more complicated, the appropriations bill that funds all education programs (elementary, secondary, and higher education) is also the same piece of legislation that provides funding for all programs at the Department of Labor and the Department of Health and Human Services (including the National Institutes of Health). One can imagine the difficult situation members of Congress are in when faced with making decisions about funding all these important programs. Often there are not enough dollars allocated to a particular funding bill to invest in all of the competing, vitally important programs. And, when Congress and the president set a goal to cut federal spending, there is even less money to direct to these programs. Therefore, the federal government has set up a zero-sum game, in which some programs will get cut just to keep other programs funded.

For the U.S. government, a fiscal year (FY) begins October 1 and ends September 30. FY10 (aka FY 2010) began in October 2009 and ended September 30, 2010.

EETT funding has not fared well in this funding environment. In 2001, its first year, EETT was funded at $700 million, close to its $1 billion authorization, but was slashed to $496 million in FY 2005 and then subsequently cut again in FYs 2006 through 2009 to $267 million. In FY 2009, the American Recovery and Reinvestment Act (ARRA) included $650 million for classroom technology and professional development through the EETT. This amount was in addition to the $267 million that was appropriated through the regular FY 2009 appropriation process. However, the actual amount funded in the appropriations process was $267 million in 2009, and in FY 2010, funding went down to $100 million. In his proposed budget for 2011, President Obama recommended that EETT not be funded as a separate program (Figure 2.1).

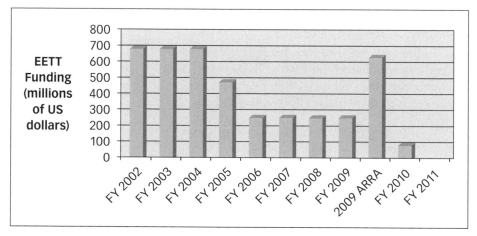

**Figure. 2.1** EETT Funding

Source: Hilary Goldmann, *The Future of Ed Tech in the Obama Administration*, a PowerPoint presentation given at the ISTE Annual Conference and Exposition, Denver, June 28, 2010.

These funding cuts meant losses of real dollars for schools. Educators tell me that schools have had to cut back on significant education technology initiatives as a result of the funding decline in the EETT program. These cuts have had direct impacts on local decision making and on the availability of resources, professional development, and tools that teachers and administrators and their students need to succeed. The EETT program is an opportunity to provide teachers and administrators with new skills and opportunities, rather than mandates and accountability measures. We must take responsibility for communicating the critical importance of these resources to policy makers in order to maintain these programs and ensure that funding is restored.

# Chapter 3

# Advocacy Success Stories

ISTE is committed to bringing the voice of educators to policy makers in terms of education technology. Through dedication, hard work, and teamwork, ISTE, its affiliated state and national organizations, and its education community members have been highly successful in influencing policy decisions at both the state and federal levels.

# Legislative Accomplishments

The following accomplishments demonstrate how the power of coalition building and grassroots mobilization can indeed make an impact:

- In 2007, ISTE influenced the Senate telecommunications bill through policy development, direct lobbying, and coalition building. ISTE proactively established an E-Rate Advisory Committee of ISTE member volunteers and charged them with developing a new set of performance measurements for the E-Rate program. These recommendations were submitted to the Federal Communications Commission and shared during direct lobbying visits with the Senate committee working on E-Rate. ISTE also shared these recommendations with the Education and Library Networks Coalition (EdLiNC). The ISTE-developed recommendations were a component of the policy debate on E-Rate performance measurements, and the final Senate committee bill included performance measurements.

- The Deleting Online Predators Act (DOPA), opposed by ISTE, was introduced in May 2006, and in almost-unheard-of speed passed the House in August 2006. DOPA would have required schools that participate in the E-Rate program to bar access by minors to commercial social networking websites or chat rooms unless used for an educational purpose with adult supervision. ISTE and others opposing DOPA worked with key U.S. senators, and this legislation never passed the Senate, and thus did not become law. As the new Congress convened in January 2007, the issue of Internet safety was still a priority, but this time the messages from the education, library, and industry community opposed to DOPA had effectively guided policy makers' approach to this important policy issue. Policy makers heard our concerns and tailored their legislative initiatives to limit as much as possible the federal intrusion and monitoring and reporting burdens on schools and libraries.

- In the waning days of the 110th Congress, legislation was passed that requires schools participating in the E-Rate program to educate students regarding appropriate behavior on social networking and chat room sites and about cyberbullying. This is a huge turnabout in congressional thinking in just a couple of years.

- In 2009, specific legislative successes include the introduction of the Achievement Through Technology and Innovation Act (ATTAIN). This legislative initiative was developed through a collaborative effort led by ISTE, the Consortium for School Networking (CoSN), the State Educational Technology Directors Association, and the Software and Information Industry Association, and was supported by most members of the education community, including the National Education Association, the National School Boards Association, and the National Association of Secondary School Principals.

  CoSN is pronounced *co-sin*.

  DOPA is pronounced *doh-pah*.

  EdLiNC is pronounced *ed-link*.

  ISTE is pronounced *iss-tee*.

- The education technology community was successful in maintaining funding for the EETT program in 2009. In fact, for FY09 the House education funding bill included a $5 million increase for EETT.

- According to ISTE's *2008–2009 Annual Report on Advocacy*, ISTE led the effort in developing a new preservice teacher education program called Preparing Teachers for Digital Age Learners (PTDAL). This program was included as part of the reauthorization of the Higher Education Act, which was signed into law in the fall of 2009. ISTE developed this program in partnership with ISTE's SIG for Teacher Educators, SIGTE.

- ISTE successfully advocated for continuation of the E-Rate program without interruption by passage of the E-Rate exemption for the Anti-Deficiency Act.

# ARRA Victories

On February 17, 2009, the American Recovery and Reinvestment Act (ARRA) was signed into law by President Obama. The act directs more than $100 billion to education. This is the largest one-time federal infusion of funds for education ever. ISTE worked closely with the Obama administration and the U.S. Congress to ensure that the ARRA included a dedicated funding stream for classroom technology and professional development through the Enhancing Education Through Technology program (EETT, Title II Part D of NCLB).

On July 27, 2010, the Senate Labor, Health and Human Services, Education, and Related Agencies Appropriations Subcommittee marked up its FY 2011 funding bill and included $100 million for the Enhancing Education Through Technology program, the same amount that was included in the House subcommittee bill. The hard work of ISTE members and the entire ed tech community, through the Ed Tech Action Network (ETAN), has most likely kept the program alive for the next year.

On August 10, 2010, President Obama signed into law a funding bill that includes $10 billion for an Education Jobs Fund. The Secretary of Education awarded funds to states that had submitted approvable applications. The funds are to be distributed under the terms of the State Fiscal Stabilization Fund. (SFSF is a one-time appropriation established by ARRA: www2.ed.gov/policy/gen/leg/recovery/factsheet/stabilization-fund.html.) The dollars will flow to local education agencies through each state's early childhood, elementary, and secondary funding formula and can be used only to retain or create education jobs for the 2010–2011 school year. Although the messaging about these funds focused on teachers' jobs, these funds can be used to save other jobs that provide educational and related services, such as instructional technology coordinators, school librarians, and social workers. Passage of the Education Jobs Fund was due in large part to the education community's unified voice and support of this measure over many months. ISTE joined with the rest of the education community in strong support of this measure.

In 2009, as part of the Administration's broadband initiative, Congress created the Broadband Technology Opportunities Program (BTOP) under ARRA. This grant program was created to promote the development and adoption of broadband throughout the United States, particularly in unserved and underserved areas. ISTE joined the Schools, Health, and Libraries Broadband (SHLB) Coalition to advance the opportunity to help connect and

SHLB is pronounced *shell-bee.*

deploy high-capacity broadband to community anchor institutions, including schools, libraries, and health care organizations.

The first round of BTOP funding in July 2009 did not fund projects that served anchor institutions. Through the SHLB Coalition, ISTE filed comments with the FCC and worked with Congress, the FCC, and the National Telecommunications and Information Administration (NTIA) to advocate for anchor institution funds for the second round. In September 2010 the program, totaling $206.8 million in grants, was approved. The new rules give schools and libraries greater flexibility to explore a variety of high-bandwidth solutions, promote greater competition among broadband providers, make more efficient use of the E-Rate fund, and open the door for meeting the National Broadband Plan goal of affordable gigabits per second (Gbps) connections to all anchor institutions in every community by 2020. The Broadband Plan's number-one goal:

> At least 100 million U.S. homes should have affordable access to actual download speeds of at least 100 megabits per second and actual upload speeds of at least 50 megabits per second. (www.broadband.gov/plan/goals-action-items.html)

# Highlights of ISTE's Advocacy Efforts

ISTE's *2009–2010 Annual Report* cited numerous success stories at the federal level. The following are highlights of ISTE's advocacy efforts.

- Convened and led 500 educators from 46 states, seven U.S. territories, and several other countries to Capitol Hill at ISTE's 2009 conference in Washington, D.C., on behalf of digital opportunities for all. The educators visited more than 290 U.S. Congressional offices in this largest-ever educational technology presence on Capitol Hill.

- Hosted the initial feedback session for the U.S. government's National Education Technology Plan at the ISTE 2009 annual conference. ISTE members provided significant input during the kickoff and continued active engagement throughout the development phase.

- Developed and launched a national campaign around the "Top Ten in '10: ISTE's Education Technology Priorities for 2010." The top ten were designed to jumpstart the dialogue and spread the word that regardless of the specific path a state, district, or school charts, educational technology is non-negotiable if lasting changes are to be made. (ISTE's top ten priorities are listed in

Chapter 5 of this booklet; the list is also available at www.iste.org/about-iste/advocacy/top-ten-in-10.aspx.)

■ Presented ISTE's first "Advocate of the Year" award to longtime ISTE member Sheryl Abshire. Later Abshire was appointed to the federal governing board of the Universal Service Administrative Company (USAC). Among its duties, the USAC oversees the E-Rate program.

■ Continuing an advisory role on the U.S. E-Rate program, ISTE filed comments on the National Broadband Plan to highlight the important role E-Rate plays in broadening access. ISTE representatives met with Federal Communications Commission and congressional staffs to discuss details of the Broadband Plan and legislation for E-Rate 2.0, successfully advocating for a broadband plan that supports a higher cap on the E-Rate and strong commitment to access for all.

■ ISTE continues to be represented on the Executive Committee of the Committee for Education Funding as co-chair of the Mission Critical Campaign and, recently, as secretary of the National Coalition for Technology in Education and Training.

■ Provided guidance and examples to ISTE members and the broader education community to assist them in applying for and receiving stimulus grants.

■ Continued to grow grassroots advocacy efforts through the Education Technology Action Network (ETAN, www.edtechactionnetwork.org). Membership in ETAN increased to more than 16,000.

■ Partnered with leading education and business associations on joint advocacy events in Washington, D.C., and on development of policy positions and reports to inform federal, state, and local policy makers (as well as other stakeholders) on the importance of technology in learning environments. Through ISTE affiliates outside the United States, direct interaction with ministries of education and other agencies, and collaborative efforts with many global partners, ISTE supports educators and policy makers in promoting relevant, technology-rich learning opportunities for young learners and for educators across the globe.

# State and Local Success Stories

In April 2007, the Louisiana Association of Computer-Using Educators (LACUE) sent a delegation to ISTE's national State Advocacy Capacity Building Conference. Attendees returned to the state galvanized and lobbied hard for educational technology funds. Their efforts resulted in the Louisiana State Legislature passing a $25 million education technology funding bill—the most technology funding from the state in the past 10 years!

### Heather Blanton, Virginia

Heather Blanton, a Title I math teacher with J. W. Adams Combined School in Pound, Virginia, is a strong proponent of technology in the classroom. She has helped lead several calls to action, encouraging legislators to preserve funding for educational technology. In 2010, ISTE presented her with its Public Policy Advocacy Trendsetter Award. Working with the Virginia Society for Technology (VSTE) as vice chairperson and director on the board of directors, Blanton's advocacy efforts have made a successful impact. For example, as a precursor to what advocacy would become in Virginia, in 2007, funding for a successful teacher resources program, which had placed 1,200 teachers in instructional technology inservice positions across the state, was in danger of being cut. Legislators wanted to slash $78 million from the program. Working with ISTE and ETAN, a VSTE advocacy committee put out a call to action. The response was overwhelming. Legislators were inundated with an enormous volume of email opposing the cuts, and teachers from around the state attended the education subcommittee meeting to make their voices heard.

- As a result of the failing economy, in 2009, education funding for computers in Virginia was on the chopping block. According to Blanton, $58 million was to be cut from the school budget. "Our bigger divisions were losing $4 to $5 million in school money," she said. "My division alone was going to lose half a million." Partnering with the Virginia alliance, they used the ETAN page to generate an email push, which coincided with webinars to generate interest. A few months later, they launched the More than Words campaign, which asked teachers to send pictures of their students using technology in the classroom. "My superintendent at the time said that he had a hard time cutting the positions when he could actually see the faces in his mind," Blanton said. "And so I thought, that's what they need to see. It's not only the value of technology, but seeing it is the difference." A final push included sending out targeted mailings, and through their advocacy efforts the governor approved about $60 million for the program. "The combined efforts of VSTE and our people fighting for education really made the difference."

■ The 2009–2010 year was an exceptionally tough budget year. Education budgets were cut overall by 8–12 percent. Specifically, the Virginia Public School Authority (VPSA) Technology Grant Program, which is roughly $60 million of state funding for providing the infrastructure for online testing, was eliminated. The total lost to larger divisions was from $4 to $6 million and $500,000 for smaller locations. To tackle this issue, an advocacy team led by the vice chair of the board of directors with members from the general membership of VSTE was put together. Members were urged to use ETAN to contact their state reps to ask them to save the funding. VSTE partnered with the Alliance for Virginia's students and the Virginia Educational Media Association to get the word out and to help with training advocates. Training sessions were conducted for state and federal issues via webinars, and to reinforce the letter-writing campaign (the More than Words campaign) which aimed to put photos of students using technology in the classroom into the hands of legislators, was re-launched. ETAN was employed again to target those involved after the budget went to the conferees and back to the governor. As a result, the VPSA Technology Grant Program not only was restored, but also received a slight increase.

Blanton continues to advocate for education in Virginia. Currently, she is fighting a battle to protect instructional technology positions and advocating for a recognized endorsement of certification in technology. She says:

*There's no incentive for getting NETS•T certified, so we're looking at possibly partnering with the Department of Education or working with them in some form. It's so valuable for teachers to have that knowledge and go through the certification process and to be able to align their teaching with it. If we can get an endorsement, then it will be an incentive for our divisions to put money toward that area.*

## Mary Wegner, Alaska

In a state twice the size of Texas and a population scattered over 656,425 square miles, reaching out and connecting students, teachers, and administrators through technology is a daunting task. But for Mary Wegner, assistant superintendent for the Sitka School District in Sitka, Alaska, the Ed Tech Action Network (ETAN) is the answer. Through Wegner's involvement as treasurer and board member of the Alaska Society for Technology in Education (ASTE), she had the opportunity to serve as an ISTE affiliate representative of the state of Alaska. "As the ISTE affiliate rep, I received the Washington Notes that Hilary Goldmann would send out, and I felt a sense of responsibility about how to share this information." As a result, she became actively involved with advocacy through the ETAN network.

According to Wegner, Alaska had always been more active on the federal than the state level, relying on the late Senator Ted Stevens to champion the state's need for subsidies and resources for education. Yet, EETT-dedicated funding at the federal level was critical, as was the E-Rate program. The E-Rate program is a huge issue in Alaska because of connectivity issues in remote areas of the state. In the far reaches of Alaska, the Internet has become as integral a part of the classroom as a blackboard and textbooks. "We rely heavily on the EETT-dedicated funding and the E-Rate," Wegner said. "Without those programs our very rural schools would not exist."

Wegner realized that connecting the ASTE membership to the ETAN network was the key to building grassroots support as well as defining ASTE's mission of advocacy for Alaska. What truly sparked the advocacy efforts was ETAN in a Box. ETAN in a Box, which enlisted volunteers to help attendees advocate for ed tech funding by crafting letters to their representatives in Congress, was launched in 2006 at ISTE's National Educational Computing Conference (NECC) in San Diego. Other state affiliates began hosting their own ETAN in a Box events. When 200 letters came in at Alaska's ASTE conference, Wegner knew she was on to something: "As soon as we started doing the ETAN in a Box, Alaska, which is the third least-populated state in the nation, became the tenth most-active ETAN state."

Building on the ETAN "Booth-in-a-Box" concept, ASTE, the largest teacher organization in the state with more than 600 members, began using its own annual conference to share awareness about ETAN. "It's a passionate, stable group," Wegner said. "You really build friendships through coming to the conferences. Members come year after year; they're a very loyal group."

## What is an ETAN Booth-in-a-Box Kit?

A large part of ETAN's success has been hard work like that of Blanton and Wegner at individual state and regional conferences. These conferences are a perfect opportunity to get out the "ed tech" community's message and continue to expand the ETAN membership. To facilitate this, ETAN has developed a "booth-in-a-box" kit that will provide some of the necessary resources to set up ETAN booths at these conferences. See Chapter 4 for more on this topic.

In addition to her work with ETAN, Wegner meets with Alaska's state legislators. According to Wegner, the letters have made a huge impact. At a recent Alaska Ed summit, one of Senator Murkowski's staffers acknowledged that ASTE "is one of the most organized, consistent groups." They always know when there's an issue because now she gets 300 letters!"

If you're new to advocacy, Wegner recommends getting involved with ETAN because it is an easy way to share your voice, but having an affiliate is a long-term way to be connected to others. "Work with your affiliate if you can because then you have the sustainability and you have the community," she said. "It's just much easier when you're one of many voices than when you think that you're the only one shouting in the wind."

Wegner previously served on the ASTE Board as treasurer and as advocacy chair. In addition to her work in Alaska, she is actively involved with ISTE, of which ASTE is an official affiliate. She has three times been appointed to serve on ISTE's Public Policy and Advocacy Committee, a group of advisers who serve as ISTE's think tank regarding policy and advocacy issues. Wegner is also one of four ISTE representatives on the ISTE/Consortium for School Networking (CoSN) Joint Policy Committee, which works to set the national policy agenda for educational technology. To help connect Alaskans' advocacy to the national effort, Wegner continues to serve as Alaska's co-chair for ETAN advocacy efforts.

At the ISTE 2010 conference in Denver, Wegner was recognized as an outstanding educational technology leader, winning the Making IT Happen award for her commitment and innovation in the field of educational technology integration in K–12 schools.

As illustrated impressively by Blanton, Wegner, and their colleagues, advocacy makes a significant impact on policy. Whether at the building, district, state, or federal level, each individual's commitment to advocate for education technology makes a difference. Not only is participation as an advocate fun and a great team-building experience, it's a great opportunity for professional growth and personal accomplishment —as you will be channeling your passion for your profession to effect positive change!

# Public Policy Advocate of the Year Award

ISTE recognizes outstanding leaders whose advocacy efforts have been evident and who have had strong impact in the field of educational technology with the Public Policy Advocate of the Year award. This award is given to an individual who has worked to expand public policy advocacy efforts for educational technology, involved others in the process, has built awareness of public policy that impacts educational technology issues and funding, and has demonstrated a strong commitment to increasing visibility and awareness of the importance of educational technology issues and funding. One individual is selected as the award winner and one is selected as the Trendsetter. Award nominations are typically accepted January through March via the ISTE website (www.iste.org/about-iste/advocacy/public-policy-award.aspx).

# Chapter 4

# Making a Difference:
# What You Can Do

*We must create our future, or we may not have one!*

*—Anita Givens, Texas Education Association*

Every American has the constitutional right to petition the government about matters of importance. Those of us in the education technology community should be proud to stand up and be counted as a special interest group. We want the president and the Congress to support policies that bring modern digital tools, content, and practices into our nation's classrooms. Influencing policy is a team effort, and sponsoring a full-time, professional lobbyist in D.C. is just one component of impacting legislation. The question becomes how do we influence policy makers to be sure that they hear and act upon our message?

A concerted, focused strategic effort to influence policy requires direct lobbying and more. Constituents' voices can be heard through a variety of means, including direct meetings with members of Congress or their staffs, congressional visits to school sites, and editorials in local newspapers, as well as email letters and faxes to members of Congress that can be generated through the Ed Tech Action Network (ETAN) website (at www.edtechactionnetwork.org).

# Direct Lobbying: Going One-on-One and Forming Coalitions

The most effective way to present your message is to meet one-on-one with policy makers—the people who have the power and influence to enact change. In addition to having offices in Washington D.C., representatives have at least one office in their district, and senators have offices throughout the state. Staffs at these offices are eager to meet with constituents locally, and will meet in the evenings or on weekends to accommodate constituents' schedules. Form a coalition of education technology advocates and hold a meeting with a local congressional staff. Your group might include a faculty member of a college or university, a teacher, an administrator, a business representative, and a community representative. Meetings like these can be powerful, excellent first steps toward building relationships with local congressional offices and getting your message to the policy makers.

If you can't make it to Washington, D.C., or your local state government offices, consider inviting policy makers to an event or to visit the school and showcase your successes and needs. You could also ask superintendents, principals, and college and university leaders to include educational technology in wish lists to legislators.

While sending email letters and faxes can be effective lobbying tools, meeting with members of Congress in person has a greater impact—attaching a name and face to an issue. Photographs of students learning with tech tools are another way of garnering a legislator's attention. A good example of this tactic in action was the More Than Words campaign conducted by the Virginia Society for Technology (VSTE), one of ISTE's affiliates, described in Chapter 3. To supplement their other advocacy efforts and emphasize the need for funding, teachers were asked to send pictures of their students using technology in the classroom. *Knowing* who is most affected if we lose technology funding is one thing, but *seeing* it makes the difference.

# Attend Town Hall Meetings

Attend a legislator's town hall meeting and ask a question or make a comment about the important role of education technology in schooling. Members of Congress regularly schedule town hall meetings in their districts. Consider attending one of these meetings, bring a group of friends, and ask a question or make a comment about education technology and the importance of continued funding for your district's students. In addition to fielding questions about other pressing current issues, it is critical for policy makers to field technology questions and to hear how significant technology is for raising student achievement and ensuring that our students can compete in today's world. Go to www.senate.gov and www.house.gov and then connect to your senators' and representatives' web pages to check out when and where they will be speaking.

# Build a Coalition

Building a coalition involves reaching out to others in your community to support education technology programs. Potential partners might include local companies, nonprofit organizations, and parent/teacher organizations. It is important to be creative—the local environmental group may want to work with you to recycle school computers!

# More Opportunities

Ed tech supporters who are not interested in or comfortable with participating in direct lobbying activities (meeting with members of Congress or their staffs) may prefer to play a significant role by drafting success stories, analyzing policy proposals, or galvanizing grassroots efforts. See which of these ways to get involved best fits your talents:

### Join the Ed Tech Action Network (ETAN)

Perhaps the easiest way to get started in advocacy is through the Ed Tech Action Network (www.edtechactionnetwork.org). ETAN is an online tool and policy resource that's powerful and easy to use. Started in 2003 by the International Society for Technology in Education (ISTE) and the Consortium for School Networking (CoSN), ETAN provides a forum for educators and others to engage in the political process and project a unified voice in support of a common cause—improving teaching and learning through the effective use of technology. ETAN's mission is to influence public policy makers at the federal, state, and local levels and to increase public investment in the competitiveness of America's classrooms and students. At the site, you'll learn how to raise awareness about vital issues with political decision makers, media, and your community; find updates about important federal legislative actions and deadlines; and receive tips for effective grassroots advocacy on the local, state, and federal levels.

## Email Letters and Faxes to Members of Congress

The ETAN network is a free website service that enables users to send email letters to members of Congress in support of education technology initiatives. It is very easy to use. Simply go to the site and type in your zip code. A prewritten draft letter will appear, and the names of your representatives will be listed. Personalize the letter by adding your own thoughts and comments, type your name and address in the area provided, and click to send the letter. It's that easy, and these letters do make a difference. As I meet with congressional staff, I hear from them about the increased communications they are receiving about education technology policy from their constituents, partly as a result of the ease of using the Internet for such communications.

## Host an ETAN Booth

Hosting an ETAN booth at an ed tech gathering or your state's conference is a great way to strengthen our voice. Mary Wegner of Alaska describes ETAN booth-in-a-box success in Chapter 3. You provide the computers, Internet access, and a couple of volunteers for the booth, and ISTE will provide you with materials and training to support your efforts.

ETAN booths are present at dozens of various affiliate conferences each year, including ISTE's annual conference. At ISTE's 2008 Conference, for example, more than 1,000 attendees passed through the booth, flooding Capitol Hill with more than 3,000 letters to support increased funding for the Enhancing Education Through Technology program. Many attendees remembered sending a letter the year before, and first-timers were pleased by how easy it is to do!

## ETAN Booth-in-a-Box Kit

Each state team will identify an individual or a committee to organize, manage, and coordinate the ETAN booth at the conference. This individual or committee will be responsible for

- ■ ensuring that the ETAN booth is supplied with computers (2 to 4 laptops are recommended) and Internet access to connect to the ETAN site.

- ■ recruiting volunteers for the ETAN booth.

- ■ providing ETAN booth space.

- ■ printing ETAN sign for booth (national team will provide electronic version).

- ■ providing content for state ETAN webpage, if requested.

- ■ printing and distributing ETAN documents at the ETAN booth.

- ■ providing feedback to the National ETAN team post-conference and mentoring/advice to other state leaders.

- ■ inserting an ETAN flyer into registration materials or doing a seat drop, if capacity allows.

- ■ providing a digital photograph of and quotation from a key education technology advocate *two weeks prior to the conference* to be posted on the ETAN homepage.

The national ETAN team will contribute

- ■ volunteer training via conference call and webinars.

- ■ written documentation for ETAN volunteers to navigate the website to facilitate letter generation.

- ■ electronic versions of ETAN documents (including electronic version of booth signage).

- ■ ETAN stickers—"My Voice was Heard. Was Yours?"

- ■ Creation of state ETAN webpage, if requested.

Source: abcs-of-advocacy.iste.wikispaces.net/ETAN+Materials

## Engage in Public Policy Development and Analysis

This means developing proposals for new programs that can be turned into legislation or reviewing legislation that has been introduced and analyzing its impact. For instance, Texas passed legislation to use state textbook money for digital resources. (For more details, see the Texas Computer Education Association, www.TCEA.org/advocacy.)

## Participate in Media Outreach

Write an op-ed for your local newspaper about the importance of educational technology in our nation's classrooms. Invite the local media (print, radio, and TV) to report on the successes as well as the existing needs in your local schools. With today's Internet social media, it only takes a minute to post a quick Facebook or Twitter update advocating for technology in education. ISTE also offers a number of ways to connect at its website through community and conference networking Nings, blogging, wikis, tweeting for Education Technology, and much more.

## Connect with Your State Affiliate

ISTE has affiliate organizations in almost every state (for a state-by-state list, see www.iste.org/membership/join-iste/affiliates/affiliates-directory.aspx). Many of these state organizations either have an advocacy committee or are in the process of developing one. This is a great way to become involved with a ready-made network of like-minded advocates who support educational technology expansion in our classrooms. Many of these organizations are becoming more vocal at both the state and federal levels.

## Attend Advocacy Training

Attend ISTE conferences and the annual Washington Education Technology Policy Summit. For more information, visit ISTE's advocacy site (www.iste.org/about-iste/advocacy.aspx).

## Stay Informed on U.S. Policy Updates

To keep up with U.S. policy activity inside the D.C. "beltway," join ISTE's Voices Carry Advocacy Committee. This group provides an informal monthly teleconference where I share updates on ed tech policy and grassroots activity. Join us and leverage your expertise to inform ISTE's policy direction. Contact me at hgoldmann@iste.org to participate in these calls.

## Share Success Stories with Policy Makers

Do you have examples of how students' test scores improve, dropout rates are reduced, or parental involvement increased, as a result of the integration of education technology? If so, sharing these successes in a one-page narrative with your policy makers and national organizations can make a difference.

It is vital that K–12 teachers and faculty who educate teachers share their success stories with policy makers. ISTE has developed an advocacy tool kit that includes examples of success stories, a template to follow when drafting success stories, and a starter kit for making your argument to a specific audience—from building and district administrators to school board representatives and state and federal policy makers. A printable copy of this tool kit is located on the CD accompanying this book and is also available for download at www.Iste.org/about-iste/advocacy/templates-and-starter-kits.aspx.

## Learn the "ABCs of Advocacy"

During ISTE's 2010 Conference and Exposition (formerly called the National Educational Computing Conference), we held a workshop called ABCs of Advocacy:

**A**dvocate,

**B**e heard,

**C**reate change!

We hope the materials in the CD accompanying this book will help to guide your advocacy efforts. On the CD you'll find the following materials developed for the workshop:

- Develop a State/Province Advocacy Plan (an advocacy story template)

- Personal Advocacy Checklist

- State/Province affiliate organization checklist (What does advocacy mean for your state/province affiliate organization?)

ISTE online resources for the "ABCs of Advocacy" include a wiki and a Ning:

- ABCs of Advocacy Wiki
  http://abcsofadvocacy2010.iste.wikispaces.net

- ABCs of Advocacy Ning
  www.iste-community.org/group/isteadvocacy/forum/topics/
  abcs-of-advocacy-and-ed-tech

After attending the workshop, Heather Blanton (Virginia Society for Technology vice chairperson and recipient of ISTE's Public Policy Advocacy Trendsetter Award) had this to say:

> I highly recommend attending an ABCs of Advocacy event at ISTE or similar sessions at your state conference. Just sitting in the room with the people for the ABCs of Advocacy at ISTE 2010 [gave me] such an overwhelming sense of "I'm not alone," as well as being around people that are as passionate as you are, who are very talented and creative and doing things in their state, which can really be inspiring to you and get you active in your own state.

## Watch the Advocacy YouTube Channel

The newest component in our advocacy arsenal is ISTE's Advocacy YouTube channel: youtube.com/user/ISTEadvocacy. Check out the videos created during the ISTE 2010 annual conference that highlight the positive effects technology is having on our students. Get inspired, shoot a video, and send it to me to post on the ISTE Advocacy channel. You can use a script similar to ours, which include the lines, "My favorite activity using technology is … " and "The impact of this activity is … " and then close with "Congress, please fund education technology." Include your name, city, and state. We tag these videos with specific policy makers' names so that the video will come up during an Internet search.

# Get Involved

Check the advocacy section of ISTE's website often for news about upcoming advocacy conferences and the latest information from inside the beltway, and take a look at the many other valuable books and resources ISTE has to offer (www.iste.org/about-iste/advocacy.aspx).

When Alaska Society for Technology in Education (ASTE) President Elect Mary Wegner was asked how volunteering for ISTE enhances her professional life, she replied:

> Volunteering for ISTE connects me to research, resources, and breaking news I can bring to my district and colleagues elsewhere in Alaska. ISTE draws people who understand the essence of good teaching and learning; being an active participant in ISTE initiatives allows me to network with some amazing individuals.

I hope this chapter has persuaded readers that federal policy does directly affect the teaching and learning that takes place in our nation's classrooms, and that each of us has the opportunity and the responsibility to, in turn, influence those federal policies. We must band together and make our voices heard.

The keys to success in any advocacy activity you embark upon is to remember that policy makers are elected to serve their constituents and that they really do want to hear from you. If not us, who? If not now, when? Together we can make a significant difference!

# Advocacy Resources

**ABCs of Advocacy online**
http://abcsofadvocacy2010.iste.wikispaces.net

> (See also the CD with this booklet for materials developed for the 2010 conference.)

**Advocacy Lounge Wiki**
http://advocacyloungeatiste2010.iste.wikispaces.net

> Visit the Advocacy Lounge to participate in activities and make your voice heard.

**Ed Tech Action Network (ETAN)**
www.edtechactionnetwork.org

**Education and Library Networks Coalition (EdLiNC)**
www.edlinc.org

**ETAN in a Box/ETAN Booth-in-a-Box**
http://abcsofadvocacy2010.iste.wikispaces.net/Section+3

**Hilary Goldmann's Blog on the ISTE Community Ning**
www.iste-community.org/profiles/blog/list?user=HilaryGoldmann

> I post updates several times a week.

**ISTE Advocacy Templates & Starter Kits**
www.iste.org/about-iste/advocacy/templates-and-starter-kits.aspx

> (See also the CD with this booklet.)

**ISTE Advocacy Web Page**
www.iste.org/about-iste/advocacy.aspx

**ISTE Advocacy YouTube Channel**
www.youtube.com/user/ISTEadvocacy

**ISTE Affiliates Global Interactive Map**
http://affiliates.iste.wikispaces.net/Directory+of+Affiliates

**ISTE Affiliates State-by-State Directory**
www.iste.org/membership/join-iste/affiliates/affiliates-directory.aspx

## ISTE Community Ning
www.iste-community.org

## ISTE Conference Ning
www.iste2012.org

## ISTE Connects Blog
www.iste.org/connect/iste-connects/blog.aspx

## ISTE on Facebook
www.facebook.com/pages/ISTE/8828374188

## ISTE Group on LinkedIn
www.linkedin.com/groupInvitation?gid=2811&sharedKey=07936D605ECB&trk=

## ISTE Membership Wikispace
www.iste.wikispaces.net

## ISTE Mobile Application
www.iste.org/connect/iste-mobile.aspx

## ISTE Policy Positions
www.iste.org/about-iste/advocacy/policy-positions.aspx

## ISTE in Second Life
www.iste.org/connect/communities/second-life.aspx

## ISTE Voices Carry Advocacy Group
www.iste-community.org/group/isteadvocacy

## ISTE Wikispaces: Advocacy & Public Relations
http://affiliates.iste.wikispaces.net/Advocacy+%26+Public+Relations

## ISTE's Top Ten in '10
www.iste.org/about-iste/advocacy/top-ten-in-10.aspx

## Ed Tech Trio for 2011: ISTE's U.S. Education Technology Priorities
www.iste.org/news/11-01-18/ISTE_Releases_Trio_of_U_S_Ed_Tech_
Priorities_for_2011.aspx

## Tweet for Education Technology
twitter.com/isteconnects

> Sign up and start "tweeting" for advocacy! Follow Hilary Goldmann on Twitter:
> @hgoldmann

## Volunteer at ISTE

www.iste.org/connect/volunteer.aspx

## Webinar: Learning How to Make Your Voice Heard

http://iste.acrobat.com/p99336231

> Webinar presented by the Advocacy Sub-Committee of the Affiliate Membership Committee

## U.S. Department of Education Policy Overview

www2.ed.gov/policy/

# Chapter 5

# The Future of Advocacy

With each new federal administration and each election cycle comes a new set of issues and challenges, and for that reason, advocacy is an ongoing effort. Working with ISTE membership and other organizations in the education and corporate communities, we were able to maintain funding for the EETT program through 2010 using a strategic and effective lobbying and grassroots effort, despite strong attempts in Congress to eliminate funding entirely. Direct contact of constituents in Senate offices coupled with lobbying efforts repeatedly saved this program, yet every year Congress has to determine how much money each program is going to receive, so every year we must fight to keep these programs alive and funded. The Obama administration advocated for No Child Left Behind/ESEA to be reauthorized to consolidate education technology into other programs.

The following is a list of important ongoing issues and ISTE's recommendations to Congress.

# Funding of EETT

The Enhancing Education Through Technology (EETT) program is absolutely vital for teacher training, hardware and software acquisition, and infrastructure development. For fully one quarter of all U.S. states, federal EETT monies have been their *sole sources* of funding to support technology in schools. For many other states, EETT provides most of their ed tech funding. The Enhancing Education Through Technology program provided funding to states and school districts to support the integration of education technology for teaching and learning. Specifically, this funding was used for professional development for teachers and administrators, implementation of data-driven decision making and individualized learning opportunities, as well as increased parental involvement and communication, among other needs. Funding for the Enhancing Education Through Technology program was slashed in recent years (FY 2006–2009) to $267 million (see Figure 2.1, page 24).

## ISTE Recommends

As of early 2011, ISTE recommended restoring funding for the Enhancing Education Through Technology (Title II-D of NCLB) program to $300 million. Additionally, teachers and students must have access to robust broadband networks to gain access to and effectively use the latest educational technologies, services, and applications.

## Future of EETT

In February 2010, President Obama introduced his proposed FY11 budget, which recommended significant changes to the Enhancing Education Through Technology (EETT) program and Elementary and Secondary Education Act (ESEA). President Obama's proposed budget eliminated funding for the EETT program in FY11 and would delete the program entirely when Congress reauthorizes ESEA sometime in the next two years. Instead of having EETT or a successor program as a separate, directed federal program, the administration's budget proposes to infuse technology throughout the 11 major funding priorities that the administration supports in a refashioned ESEA. In April 2011, EETT was completely cut from the federal budget.

Although the proposed budget would increase FY11 funding for the Department of Education by 6.2 percent ($4.5 billion) to a total of $50.7 billion, most major federal education programs (Title I, Special Education, Teacher Quality block grants) would not receive any increases in funds. Most of the proposed additional monies would be steered to new programs and additional competitions for the Race to the Top (R2T) and Investing in Innovation (i3) programs. (See Figure 2.1, EETT Funding.)

# Achievement Through Technology and Innovation Act (ATTAIN)

As mentioned in Chapter 2, the ATTAIN Act was designed to revamp and replace the EETT program by building on its successes and focusing resources on those practices known to leverage technology for educational improvement most effectively. ATTAIN calls not only for renewed funding for hardware and software in schools, but also for focusing funds on continued professional development of teachers and school leaders in integrating such technology into instruction.

## ISTE Recommends

ISTE has recommended passing the Achievement Through Technology and Innovation Act (ATTAIN) as part of the reauthorization of the Elementary and Secondary Education Act or as a stand-alone measure. A coalition of organizations, including ISTE, sent a letter on March 26, 2010, to George Miller, Chairman, and John Kline, Ranking Member of the Education and Labor Committee, in the United States House of Representatives. The letter stated that the ATTAIN Act would update the existing EETT program by:

- Increasing the share of state-to-local funding distributed by formula from 50% to 60% and adding a minimum grant size to assure district allocations are of sufficient size to have impact.

- Strengthening teacher skills and effectiveness by raising the professional development set-aside from 25% to 40% and emphasizing the importance of timely and ongoing training.

- Channeling competitive grants to schools and districts for systemic school reform built around the use of technology for innovative redesign of the curriculum, instruction, assessment and use of data.

- Giving competitive grant priority to schools identified as in need of improvement, including those with a large share of limited English proficient students and students with disabilities.

- Focusing formula grants on students and subjects where proficiency is most lacking.

- Further ensuring that students are technologically literate by the eighth grade through state assessment, including through embedding items in other state tests.

## Future of ATTAIN

The ATTAIN Act was introduced in the House and Senate during the 110th Congress with strong bipartisan support and was included in both the House and Senate draft reauthorization packages. The passage of ATTAIN would be a significant victory for the education technology community and a testament to the power of our coalition building, networking, policy development, and member input and lobbying efforts.

# E-Rate

Since its inception in 1998, the Universal Service Schools and Libraries E-Rate program has played a major role in increasing public school classroom Internet connections. It is a U.S. government program that enables schools and libraries to purchase telecommunications and Internet service at a discounted rate. The E-Rate has also helped low-income, minority, and rural students gain near-equal broadband technology access in their classrooms as is found in other classrooms around the country. Despite an impressive track record—more than 90 percent of the nation's classrooms have Internet connectivity as a result of the program—E-Rate's mission is incomplete. Although nearly all classrooms are now connected, many have inadequate bandwidth to meet instructional needs.

## ISTE Recommends

ISTE recommends increasing E-Rate's funding cap and permanently exempting E-Rate from the Anti-Deficiency Act. The $2.25 billion annual E-Rate funding cap has never been raised and has long been inadequate to meet applicants' need. Each year, more than 30,000 applicants seek funding, and total demand normally exceeds $4 billion, outstripping available funding by approximately $1.75 billion annually. Additionally, with telecommunications/Internet access demands continuing to grow under the current cap, E-Rate may soon be unable to fund fully any internal connec tions support requests.

## E-Rate's Current Status

A September 2010 Federal Communications Commission (FCC) ruling changed the E-Rate program in several ways. ISTE has been advocating for some of the revisions, but other revisions raise concerns. ISTE issued a statement about the ruling as part of the Education and Library Networks Coalition (EdLiNC), an organization in which ISTE plays a leadership role. The statement reads: "EdLiNC wholeheartedly supports many of the changes that today's order adopts, including rule changes to streamline the E-Rate application process and to make leased dark fiber eligible for discount, but we remain extremely concerned that the Commission has yet to adequately address the biggest problem facing the program: lack of funding." (The term "dark fiber" is used to describe fiber-optic strands that are not being used or have no equipment being used on the ends of the fiber.)

The FCC ruling adjusts E-Rate's funding cap annually in accordance with inflation. The government caps funding for the program at $2.25 billion and has done so for a decade. Although this is a significant amount, data show that the demand for the program far exceeds the cap. The FCC's ruling to adjust the cap based on inflation is a step in the right direction, but funding is still far below the demand and need.

These new rules allow the leasing of fiber optics as an eligible Priority 1 service (Internet access) and allow applicants to lease dark fiber or lit fiber optics (lit fiber is an active fiber-optic strand) from the most cost-effective provider, including but not limited to telecommunications carriers and others, such as research education networks; regional, state, and local government entities or networks; nonprofit and for-profit providers; and utility companies. This change provides more options and flexibility for schools and may lower their costs.

This change in the new rules makes permanent a waiver that lets schools allow community members to use E-Rate services outside of school hours, and it creates an off-campus wireless connectivity pilot program to "investigate the merits and challenges of wireless off-premises connectivity services and to help the Commission determine whether and how these services should ultimately be eligible for E-Rate support" (www.fcc.gov/ftp/Daily_Releases/Daily_Business/2010/db1108/DA-10-2128A1.txt).

Although ISTE wholeheartedly supports school-to-home connectivity, there are concerns about creating new programs and new eligible services under the E-Rate program without significant investment of additional funding to pay for them. The ruling also streamlines the application process, removing the technology-plan requirement for Priority 1 services. However, applicants who request Priority 2 funding (for internal connections and basic maintenance) must still complete a technology plan. (See www.fcc.gov/learnnet and www.edlinc.org for more information on E-Rate.)

## Future of E-Rate

In the congressional sessions 2002–2009, Congress passed and the president signed legislation to temporarily exempt E-Rate and all of universal service from the Anti-Deficiency Act. (The ADA prevents Congress from allowing expenditures in excess of amounts appropriated.) The last ADA exemption expired on December 31, 2010, and, without the enactment of an additional temporary exemption or a permanent exemption, the E-Rate program would have faced another shutdown with major disruption for schools and libraries. Congress passed and the president signed another one-year extension averting another shutdown.

# Preparing Teachers for Digital Age Learners (PTDAL)

To improve teaching and learning, it is critical that preservice teachers be fully trained and prepared to use technology and integrate it into their curricula before they set foot in a classroom. To ensure that America has the most technologically savvy educator workforce in the world, the Preparing Teachers for Digital Age Learners (PTDAL) program supports preservice teachers by funding innovative preservice grants to institutions of higher education.

## ISTE Recommends

ISTE recommends funding the Preparing Teachers for Digital Age Learners (PTDAL) program at $100 million.

ISTE strongly supports the Preparing Teachers for Digital Age Learners (PTDAL) program under Title II of the Higher Education Act. The PTDAL program, which was included in the 2008 reauthorization of the Higher Education Act, could provide a significant boost to ensuring that our nation's new teachers have the skills and know-how to effectively integrate modern digital tools and content into classroom learning.

## Future of PTDAL

The Obama administration's FY11 Budget Proposal provides no funding for PTDAL.

# National Educational Technology Standards (NETS)

Since 1998, ISTE's NETS have served as a roadmap for improved learning and teaching. They help measure proficiency and set goals for what students (NETS•S), teachers (NETS•T), and administrators (NETS•A) should know and be able to do with technology in education. Our proven leadership in developing benchmarks and guiding implementation has resulted in broad adoption of ISTE's standards in the United States and many other countries (www.iste.org/about-iste.aspx).

## ISTE Recommends

ISTE recommends adopting the National Educational Technology Standards into legislation.

Because administrators at the local level ensure that technology investments and professional development align to curriculum standards set by their district and state, data-driven decision making among administrators and teachers is key in this process. Useful data on student achievement can identify gaps where students are not meeting curriculum standards. By identifying teachers' needs for classroom and building technologies, administrators can ensure that funding is targeted where it will be most efficient and effective.

# Top Ten in '10

Through a common focus on boosting student achievement and closing the achievement gap, policy makers and educators alike are now reiterating their commitment to the sorts of programs and instructional efforts that can have maximum effects on instruction and student outcomes.

This commitment requires a keen understanding of past accomplishments and strategies for future success. Regardless of the specific improvement paths a state or school district may chart, the use of technology in teaching and learning is nonnegotiable if we are to make real and lasting change.

With the Race to the Top (RttT; R2T) and Investing in Innovation (i3) awards in 2010, states and school districts saw increased attention on educational improvement, backed by financial support through these grants.

In 2010, ISTE identified the following 10 priorities essential for making good on this commitment. (ISTE's Top Ten in '10 is also available for download at www.iste.org/about-iste/advocacy/top-ten-in-10.aspx.)

1.  **Establish technology in education as the backbone of school improvement.** To truly improve our schools for the long term and ensure that all students are equipped with the knowledge and skills necessary to achieve in the 21st century, education technology must permeate every corner of the learning process. From years of research, we know that technology can serve as a primary driver for systemic school improvement, including school leadership, an improved learning culture, and excellence in professional practice. We must ensure that technology is at the foundation of current education reform efforts and is explicit and clear in its role, mission, and expected impact.

2.  **Leverage education technology as a gateway for college and career readiness.** In 2009, President Obama established a national goal of producing the highest percentage of college graduates in the world by the year 2020. To achieve this goal in the next 10 years, we must embrace new instructional approaches that both increase the college-going rates and the high school graduation rates. By effectively engaging students as they learn through technology, teachers can demonstrate the relevance of 21st-century education, keeping more children in the pipeline as they pursue a rigorous, interesting, and pertinent PK–12 public education.

3.  **Ensure technology expertise is infused throughout our schools and classrooms.** In addition to providing all teachers with digital tools and content, we must ensure technology experts are integrated throughout all schools, particularly as we increase focus and priority on STEM (science-technology-engineering-mathematics) instruction and expand distance and online learning opportunities for students. Just as we prioritize reading and math experts, so, too, must we place a premium on technology experts who can help the entire school maximize its resources and opportunities. To support these experts, as

well as all educators who integrate technology into the overall curriculum, we must substantially increase our support for the federal Enhancing Education Through Technology (EETT) program. EETT provides critical support for on-going professional development, implementation of data-driven decision making, personalized learning opportunities, and increased parental involvement. EETT should be increased to $500 million in FY 2011.

4. Continuously upgrade educators' classroom technology skills as a prerequisite of highly effective teaching. As part of our nation's continued push to ensure every classroom is led by a qualified, highly effective teacher, we must commit that all P–12 educators have the skills to use modern information tools and digital content to support student learning in content areas and for student assessment. Effective teachers in the 21st century should be, by definition, technologically savvy teachers.

5. Invest in preservice education technology. Teacher preparation is one of the most important aspects of a world-class, 21st-century system of education and learning. A federal investment in a new, technology-savvy generation of teachers is critical. To ensure their success in the classroom, preservice teachers must be prepared to use technology and integrate it into the curricula before their first day as a teacher of record. By fully funding programs such as Preparing Teachers for Digital Age Learners (PTDAL), we can ensure that the United States produces the most technologically savvy educator workforce in the world.

6. Leverage technology to scale improvement. Through federal initiatives such as i3 grants, school districts across the nation are being asked to scale up current school improvement efforts to maximize reach and impact. School districts that have successfully led school turnarounds and improvement efforts recognize that education technology is one of the best ways to accelerate reform, providing the immediate tools to ensure that all teachers and students have access to the latest innovative instructional pathways. If we are serious about school improvement, we must be serious about education technology.

7. Provide high-speed broadband for all. The connectivity divide may be the most critical aspect of both our digital divide and our learning divide over the next decade. We must continue our national commitment to ensuring broadband access for all students through initiatives such as the E-Rate program. Today's classroom applications require significant bandwidth that many schools lack. Students who don't have Internet access at home face a significant hurdle to participate in school assignments and produce high quality schoolwork—and

their parents are hindered in school-to-home communications. We must provide high-speed bandwidth to our nation's classrooms and focus on the school-to-home connection so that all students can succeed.

8. Boost student learning through data and assessment efforts. In schools across the nation, teachers, principals, and district administrators are increasingly discovering the benefits of real-time instructional and curriculum management systems. To maximize these efforts, we must provide educators with the systems, knowledge, and support they need to effectively tailor their teaching strategies and better meet the individual needs of each learner. Teachers' capabilities to use data to improve instruction are equally important to contemporary data and assessment systems.

9. Invest in ongoing research and development. With the current push for both innovation and school improvement, it is essential that we, as a nation, invest in the research and development necessary to identify what is driving increased student achievement and why. Increased investment in education R&D, particularly with regard to innovation in teaching and learning, ensures that we remain a global leader in education. By stimulating meaningful, broad-based research and the dissemination of such research, we can ensure that the quality of teaching and learning in our classrooms keeps up with the goals and expectations we set for our students.

10. Promote global digital citizenship. In recent years, we have seen the walls that divide nations and economies come down and, of necessity, we've become focused on an increasingly competitive and flat world. Education technology is the great equalizer in this environment, breaking down artificial barriers to effective teaching and learning and providing new reasons and opportunities for collaboration. Our children are held to greater scrutiny when it comes to learning and achievement compared with their fellow students overseas. We, in turn, must ensure that all students have access to the best learning technologies.

For educators, these issues are paramount to improving the instructional process and boosting achievement for all students. As federal, state, and local policy makers focus on RttT, i3, the FY 2011 budget, and Elementary and Secondary Education Act (ESEA) reauthorization, these issues must form the backbone of the discussion.

Today, the nation and the world face challenges that seem equally insurmountable, ranging from combating global warming to adjusting to the flattening of the global marketplace. To overcome these challenges, the nation must continue to invest in education—and more specifically, the kind of education that will arm our students with the skills, creativity, and know-how to achieve in the 21st century.

Technology is critical for moving the U.S. education system into the digital age. It is also important that we use robust broadband connectivity to learn and work as 21st-century professionals so that we can remain competitive in the emerging world economy. Education can and must adapt to meet the expectations, needs, and potential of this and coming generations.

ISTE will continue to work with the Obama administration and Congress to highlight the opportunities that ed tech provides to meet the president's goals of producing the highest percentage of college graduates in the world by 2020 and closing the achievement gap so that all students have the opportunity to succeed. Yet, to achieve these goals it is vital for the policy makers not only to hear the voices of ISTE and its coalition partners, but also to listen to the voices of the people within the education community.

Funding cuts are always a concern for educational technology, both at the state and federal levels, but you can proactively influence the decision-making process and shape the future. Take the next step to becoming an ed tech advocate. Get involved with your state affiliate organization, join the advocacy committee—and if there isn't one, start one. Strengthen your advocacy expertise by utilizing the tools and resources in this guide. Take advantage of today's web and social media channels to unleash the power of people!

And remember, ISTE is here to partner with you and to help you on your advocacy journey.

# An Ed Tech Trio for 2011

If 2010 was the year of education reform, 2011 has shaped up as the year of getting back to education basics. On January 18, 2011, ISTE released its U.S. Technology Priorities (www.iste.org/news/11-01-18/ISTE_RELEASES_2011_U_S_EDUCATION_TECHNOLOGY_PRIORITIES.aspx). This press release appears below. The unabridged trio of priorities appears in the Conclusion.

> With both the White House and the U.S. Congress identifying education as a top policy priority for 2011, the International Society for Technology in Education (ISTE) today released its "Ed Tech Trio for

2011," identifying the top three education issues central to strengthening schools, instruction, and U.S. competitiveness.

An Ed Tech Trio for 2011: ISTE's U.S. Education Technology Priorities includes:

- Continued federal technology investment in existing ed tech programs such as Enhancing Education Through Technology (EETT) and the Preparing Teachers for Digital Age Learners Act (PTDAL);

- Recognition that education technology is central to successful school improvement efforts, including teacher and principal quality and school turnaround, and must be included as part of federal policy and funding priorities; and

- Closing the digital divide by following through on efforts to provide all students with access to broadband as well as Internet access to educational materials outside of school hours.

# Conclusion

*We need to do more than tinker around the edges of school reform. If we're really serious about strengthening U.S. schools and helping our students to compete in a global economy, we must make a serious commitment to education technology. Countries around the world recognize the essential role ed tech plays in school improvement and student success. Let's require ed tech as a component in all ongoing school improvement efforts. Opportunities expand in digital environments. Let's leverage that in policy and in the classroom.*

*—Don Knezek, ISTE CEO*

# The Future of Ed Tech Advocacy

ISTE will continue to champion policies at the federal, state, and local levels that promote the effective implementation of digital tools and content into teaching and learning.

ISTE's advocacy initiatives bring the voice of local educators to the nation's policy makers. At the same time, ISTE is developing advocacy expertise among educators, empowering them to be valuable informational resources for policy makers at all levels of government. Yet, few policy makers recognize the positive impacts technology has had on our students and our schools. As educators, we have not shared our success stories often enough or persuasively enough with elected officials. As these officials begin to hear more from us about the positive effects of technology on curriculum, student success, and educational opportunities, they will be likely to increase support for technology use in schools. Each of us has the capability to be an advocate for improved teaching and learning with technology.

Despite the significant political changes coming to the education field, one thing is certain: education technology remains an absolutely essential component in strengthening our public schools, improving the quality of education for all students, and providing the skills and knowledge all learners need for both school and career success. The great equalizer in our efforts to close the achievement gap and improve our schools, ed tech serves as a vital school improvement tool.

## Ed Tech Trio

ISTE has identified three education issues that policy makers should be considering. ISTE members will continue to rally around these three education priorities:

1. **Dedicated Ed Tech Funding Leads to Student Success**—Federal vision and leadership is needed to ensure all of our nation's students are educated in schools that meet the needs of 21st-century learners. To meet these goals, direct federal technology investment in existing federal programs—such as the Enhancing Education Through Technology (EETT) program and the Preparing Teachers for Digital Age Learners Act (PTDAL)—is required. In 2010, recognizing the invaluable role ed tech plays in our K–12 system, the Obama Administration pledged to integrate education technology into all corners of ESEA. While ed tech is indeed central to a 21st-century education, real academic progress through technology cannot be achieved if federal funding for technology is diffused among all major education programs and a

proven program like EETT is defunded in that process. Like reading, math, and other core components of the instructional process, ed tech requires a dedicated funding stream and a long term commitment to yield results.

2. **Technology in Education Remains the Backbone of School Improvement**—To truly improve our schools for the long term and ensure that all students are equipped with the knowledge and skills necessary to achieve in the digital age, education technology must permeate every corner of the teaching and learning process. In 2010, the United States invested significant taxpayer dollars in programs such as Race to the Top (RttT) and Investing in Innovation (i3). If we are to maximize these and other federal reform efforts, we must collectively recognize that ed tech is the backbone of school improvement. Whether it be teacher and principal quality, the turnaround of low-performing schools, improved data tracking and utilization, or the adoption and implementation of stronger academic standards and online assessments, education technology is central to lasting improvement. Educators and ed tech advocates remain committed to helping policy makers understand the clear role, mission, and expected impact ed tech can have on K–12 education.

3. **Broadband for All Is a National Priority**—The United States must continue its national commitment to closing the digital divide by working to provide all students access to broadband and the virtually limitless information and learning tools resulting from it. Today's students and teachers are increasingly relying on broadband for everyday classroom needs. School and district networks are barely keeping pace with these increased demands. As online learning and online assessments become more commonplace (including the 2014 deadline for many states to move to online assessments) many school district networks will be at the breaking point. Students also need Internet access at home, as successful completion of school assignments often demands access to broadband. Students who do not have Internet access at home are at a significant disadvantage. As policy makers re-visit existing telecommunications law they must continue their commitment to the E-Rate program to ensure districts can develop robust networks. Policy makers must also ensure that all of our students have Internet access to educational materials outside of school hours.

As a unified trio, these three priorities represent the future of education in the 21st century. Whether it is ESEA reauthorization, the adoption of Common Core Standards, the development of common assessments, or the identification of education budget priorities in what will likely be a difficult FY 2012 budget, education technology is the strongest investment policy makers can make in our classrooms. A dedicated, long-term financial commitment to ed tech can improve our schools, boost student achievement, and deliver real return on investment in our classrooms.

*I hope this booklet has provided you with some insights into current education technology policy and some steps to take to become involved in advocacy. Together our voices carry!*

*—Hilary Goldmann*

*Twitter @hgoldmann*
*twitter.com/isteconnects*
*Email*
*hgoldmann@iste.org*

# Appendix

# NETS for Students, Teachers, and Administrators

ISTE published the original National Educational Technology Standards (NETS) for students, teachers, and administrators in 1998, 2000, and 2001, respectively. The NETS, now used in every U.S. state and many other countries, are credited with significantly influencing expectations for students and creating targets of excellence related to technology. In 2009, ISTE completed the next generation of NETS, which provide a roadmap of global digital age skills for learning, teaching, and leadership. The updated ("refreshed") student standards (NETS•S) were released in 2007, NETS for Teachers (NETS•T) in 2008, and NETS for Administrators (NETS•A) in 2009.

# National Educational Technology Standards for Students (NETS•S)

All K–12 students should be prepared to meet the following standards and performance indicators.

## 1. Creativity and Innovation

Students demonstrate creative thinking, construct knowledge, and develop innovative products and processes using technology. Students:

a. apply existing knowledge to generate new ideas, products, or processes

b. create original works as a means of personal or group expression

c. use models and simulations to explore complex systems and issues

d. identify trends and forecast possibilities

## 2. Communication and Collaboration

Students use digital media and environments to communicate and work collaboratively, including at a distance, to support individual learning and contribute to the learning of others. Students:

a. interact, collaborate, and publish with peers, experts, or others employing a variety of digital environments and media

b. communicate information and ideas effectively to multiple audiences using a variety of media and formats

c. develop cultural understanding and global awareness by engaging with learners of other cultures

d. contribute to project teams to produce original works or solve problems

## 3. Research and Information Fluency

Students apply digital tools to gather, evaluate, and use information. Students:

a. plan strategies to guide inquiry

**b.** locate, organize, analyze, evaluate, synthesize, and ethically use information from a variety of sources and media

**c.** evaluate and select information sources and digital tools based on the appropriateness to specific tasks

**d.** process data and report results

## 4. Critical Thinking, Problem Solving, and Decision Making

Students use critical-thinking skills to plan and conduct research, manage projects, solve problems, and make informed decisions using appropriate digital tools and resources. Students:

**a.** identify and define authentic problems and significant questions for investigation

**b.** plan and manage activities to develop a solution or complete a project

**c.** collect and analyze data to identify solutions and make informed decisions

**d.** use multiple processes and diverse perspectives to explore alternative solutions

## 5. Digital Citizenship

Students understand human, cultural, and societal issues related to technology and practice legal and ethical behavior. Students:

**a.** advocate and practice the safe, legal, and responsible use of information and technology

**b.** exhibit a positive attitude toward using technology that supports collaboration, learning, and productivity

**c.** demonstrate personal responsibility for lifelong learning

**d.** exhibit leadership for digital citizenship

### 6. Technology Operations and Concepts

Students demonstrate a sound understanding of technology concepts, systems, and operations. Students:

**a.** understand and use technology systems

**b.** select and use applications effectively and productively

**c.** troubleshoot systems and applications

**d.** transfer current knowledge to the learning of new technologies

*© 2007 International Society for Technology in Education (ISTE), www.iste.org. All rights reserved.*

# National Educational Technology Standards for Teachers (NETS•T)

All classroom teachers should be prepared to meet the following standards and performance indicators.

## 1. Facilitate and Inspire Student Learning and Creativity

Teachers use their knowledge of subject matter, teaching and learning, and technology to facilitate experiences that advance student learning, creativity, and innovation in both face-to-face and virtual environments. Teachers:

a. promote, support, and model creative and innovative thinking and inventiveness

b. engage students in exploring real-world issues and solving authentic problems using digital tools and resources

c. promote student reflection using collaborative tools to reveal and clarify students' conceptual understanding and thinking, planning, and creative processes

d. model collaborative knowledge construction by engaging in learning with students, colleagues, and others in face-to-face and virtual environments

## 2. Design and Develop Digital-Age Learning Experiences and Assessments

Teachers design, develop, and evaluate authentic learning experiences and assessments incorporating contemporary tools and resources to maximize content learning in context and to develop the knowledge, skills, and attitudes identified in the NETS•S. Teachers:

a. design or adapt relevant learning experiences that incorporate digital tools and resources to promote student learning and creativity

b. develop technology-enriched learning environments that enable all students to pursue their individual curiosities and become active participants in setting their own educational goals, managing their own learning, and assessing their own progress

c. customize and personalize learning activities to address students' diverse learning styles, working strategies, and abilities using digital tools and resources

d. provide students with multiple and varied formative and summative assessments aligned with content and technology standards and use resulting data to inform learning and teaching

## 3. Model Digital-Age Work and Learning

Teachers exhibit knowledge, skills, and work processes representative of an innovative professional in a global and digital society. Teachers:

a. demonstrate fluency in technology systems and the transfer of current knowledge to new technologies and situations

b. collaborate with students, peers, parents, and community members using digital tools and resources to support student success and innovation

c. communicate relevant information and ideas effectively to students, parents, and peers using a variety of digital-age media and formats

d. model and facilitate effective use of current and emerging digital tools to locate, analyze, evaluate, and use information resources to support research and learning

## 4. Promote and Model Digital Citizenship and Responsibility

Teachers understand local and global societal issues and responsibilities in an evolving digital culture and exhibit legal and ethical behavior in their professional practices. Teachers:

a. advocate, model, and teach safe, legal, and ethical use of digital information and technology, including respect for copyright, intellectual property, and the appropriate documentation of sources

b. address the diverse needs of all learners by using learner-centered strategies and providing equitable access to appropriate digital tools and resources

c. promote and model digital etiquette and responsible social interactions related to the use of technology and information

d. develop and model cultural understanding and global awareness by engaging with colleagues and students of other cultures using digital-age communication and collaboration tools

## 5. Engage in Professional Growth and Leadership

Teachers continuously improve their professional practice, model lifelong learning, and exhibit leadership in their school and professional community by promoting and demonstrating the effective use of digital tools and resources. Teachers:

a. participate in local and global learning communities to explore creative applications of technology to improve student learning

b. exhibit leadership by demonstrating a vision of technology infusion, participating in shared decision making and community building, and developing the leadership and technology skills of others

c. evaluate and reflect on current research and professional practice on a regular basis to make effective use of existing and emerging digital tools and resources in support of student learning

d. contribute to the effectiveness, vitality, and self-renewal of the teaching profession and of their school and community

# National Educational Technology Standards for Administrators (NETS•A)

All school administrators should be prepared to meet the following standards and performance indicators.

## 1. Visionary Leadership

Educational Administrators inspire and lead development and implementation of a shared vision for comprehensive integration of technology to promote excellence and support transformation throughout the organization. Educational Administrators:

**a.** inspire and facilitate among all stakeholders a shared vision of purposeful change that maximizes use of digital-age resources to meet and exceed learning goals, support effective instructional practice, and maximize performance of district and school leaders

**b.** engage in an ongoing process to develop, implement, and communicate technology-infused strategic plans aligned with a shared vision

**c.** advocate on local, state, and national levels for policies, programs, and funding to support implementation of a technology-infused vision and strategic plan

## 2. Digital-Age Learning Culture

Educational Administrators create, promote, and sustain a dynamic, digital-age learning culture that provides a rigorous, relevant, and engaging education for all students. Educational Administrators:

**a.** ensure instructional innovation focused on continuous improvement of digital-age learning

**b.** model and promote the frequent and effective use of technology for learning

**c.** provide learner-centered environments equipped with technology and learning resources to meet the individual, diverse needs of all learners

**d.** ensure effective practice in the study of technology and its infusion across the curriculum

**e.** promote and participate in local, national, and global learning communities that stimulate innovation, creativity, and digital-age collaboration

## 3. Excellence in Professional Practice

Educational Administrators promote an environment of professional learning and innovation that empowers educators to enhance student learning through the infusion of contemporary technologies and digital resources. Educational Administrators:

**a.** allocate time, resources, and access to ensure ongoing professional growth in technology fluency and integration

**b.** facilitate and participate in learning communities that stimulate, nurture, and support administrators, faculty, and staff in the study and use of technology

**c.** promote and model effective communication and collaboration among stakeholders using digital-age tools

**d.** stay abreast of educational research and emerging trends regarding effective use of technology and encourage evaluation of new technologies for their potential to improve student learning

## 4. Systemic Improvement

Educational Administrators provide digital-age leadership and management to continuously improve the organization through the effective use of information and technology resources. Educational Administrators:

**a.** lead purposeful change to maximize the achievement of learning goals through the appropriate use of technology and media-rich resources

**b.** collaborate to establish metrics, collect and analyze data, interpret results, and share findings to improve staff performance and student learning

**c.** recruit and retain highly competent personnel who use technology creatively and proficiently to advance academic and operational goals

    **d.** establish and leverage strategic partnerships to support systemic improvement

    **e.** establish and maintain a robust infrastructure for technology including integrated, interoperable technology systems to support management, operations, teaching, and learning

## 5. Digital Citizenship

Educational Administrators model and facilitate understanding of social, ethical, and legal issues and responsibilities related to an evolving digital culture. Educational Administrators:

    **a.** ensure equitable access to appropriate digital tools and resources to meet the needs of all learners

    **b.** promote, model, and establish policies for safe, legal, and ethical use of digital information and technology

    **c.** promote and model responsible social interactions related to the use of technology and information

    **d.** model and facilitate the development of a shared cultural understanding and involvement in global issues through the use of contemporary communication and collaboration tools

# Glossary of Abbreviations

**ADA.** Anti-Deficiency Act

**ARRA.** American Recovery and Reinvestment Act—often called the Recovery Act or the Stimulus

**ATTAIN.** Achievement Through Technology and Innovation Act

**CoSN.** Consortium for School Networking: www.cosn.org

**DOPA.** Deleting Online Predators Act (of 2006)

**EdLINC.** Education and Library Networks Coalition: www.edlinc.org

**EETT or E2T2.** Enhancing Education Through Technology program, Title II, Part D of The No Child Left Behind Act (of 2001)

**ESEA.** Elementary and Secondary Education Act (of 1965), reauthorized by the No Child Left Behind Act of 2001

**ETAN.** Ed Tech Action Network: www.edtechactionnetwork.org

**FCC.** Federal Communications Commission: www.fcc.gov

**FY.** Fiscal year (for the U.S. government, October 1 through September 30)

**i3.** Investing in Innovation

**IDEA.** Individuals with Disabilities Education Act (of 2004), the amended version of the Education for All Handicapped Children Act of 1975; final regulations passed in 2006

**ISTE.** International Society for Technology in Education: www.iste.org

**LEA.** Local education agencies

**NCLB.** The No Child Left Behind Act

**NETS.** National Educational Technology Standards: www.iste.org/nets

**NTIA.** National Telecommunications and Information Administration

**PT³ program.** Preparing Tomorrow's Teachers to Use Technology program (of 1998), replaced by the PTDAL program

**PTDAL.** Preparing Teachers for Digital Age Learners program

**R&D.** Research and development

**RttT or R2T.** Race to the Top fund (authorized by the American Recovery and Reinvestment Act of 2009)

**RTTA.** Race to the Top Assessment program (authorized by the American Recovery and Reinvestment Act of 2009)

**SETDA.** State Educational Technology Directors Association: www.setda.org

**SFSF.** State Fiscal Stabilization Fund (established by the American Recovery and Reinvestment Act of 2009)

**SHLB.** Schools, Health & Libraries Broadband Coalition: www.shlbc.org

**SIIA.** Software & Information Industry Association: www.siia.net

**SIG.** Special interest group

**STEM.** Science, technology, engineering, and mathematics

**USAC.** Universal Service Administrative Company (not-for-profit corporation that, among other things, oversees the E-Rate program)

**USF.** Universal Service Fund (administered by USAC)

**WAN.** Wide-area network

# Bibliography

Bernstein, J. (2010, October). Congress adjourns for the elections without completing any FY11 funding bills. *Washington Notes*. In *ISTE Community Ning*, by H. Goldmann. Retrieved October 18, 2010, from www.iste-community.org/profiles/blogs/congress-adjourns-october

Consortium for School Networking (CoSN). (2011, April 15). What Education & Industry Leaders Are Saying About the Elimination of Funding for the Enhancing Technology Through Education (EETT) Program in the FY 2011 Appropriations Bill. [Press release.] Retrieved May 6, 2011, from www.cosn.org/Default.aspx?tabid=8059&ctl=ArticleView&mid=11601&articleId=792

Ed Tech Action Network (ETAN). (2010). Sustain EETT funding in FY11 and infuse technology into ESEA rewrite. In Key legislation and agency proceedings. Retrieved October 10, 2010, from www.edtechactionnetwork.org/key-legislation

Ed Tech Coalition. (2010). EETT funding history. A chart in *Support $500 million for Enhancing Education Through Technology (EETT) program in FY11*. Available at c0457741.cdn.cloudfiles.rackspacecloud.com/Support_Funding_of_500_million_for_FY2011.pdf

Ed Tech Coalition. (n.d.). ESEA Coalition recommendations. Support both a separate ed tech program like ATTAIN and the infusion of technology throughout ESEA.

Ed Tech Coalition. (n.d.). E-Rate Coalition recommendations. Increase the e-rate's funding cap and permanently exempt e-rate from the Anti-Deficiency Act.

Education and Library Networks Coalition (EdLiNC). (2007, February). *E-Rate: 10 years of connecting kids and community*. (A joint report of EdLiNC and NCTET). Retrieved May 5, 2011, from www.edlinc.org/resources.html#edlincpubs

Education and Library Networks Coalition (EdLiNC). (2010). E-Rate. *Get the Facts*. Retrieved October 25, 2010, from www.edlinc.org/get_facts.html

Federal Communications Commission. (2010). *National broadband plan: Goals & action items*. Retrieved May 3, 2011, from www.broadband.gov/plan/goals-action-items.html

Federal Communications Commission. (2010, September 28). *Upgrading E-Rate for the 21st century* (FCC 10-175). Available at www.fcc.gov/Daily_Releases/Daily_Business/2010/db1001/FCC-10-175A1.pdf

Federal Communications Commission. (2010, November 8). *Wireline Competition Bureau announces application deadline for the E-Rate deployed ubiquitously (EDU) 2011 pilot program*. Available at www.fcc.gov/ftp/Daily_Releases/Daily_Business/2010/db1108/DA-10-2128A1.txt

Federal Communications Commission. (2011). *E-Rate*. Retrieved May 3, 2011, from www.fcc.gov/learnnet

Goldmann, H. (2006–2010). *Voices Carry* online newsletter columns. *Leading & Learning with Technology*. Eugene, OR: International Society for Technology in Education. Available from www.iste.org

Goldmann, H. (2007, October). Educational technology policy: Educators influencing the process. In *Yearbook of the National Society for the Study of Education* (Vol. 106, Issue 2, pp. 133–146). New York, NY: Teachers College, Columbia University. Available at http://onlinelibrary.wiley.com/doi/10.1111/ysse.2007.106.issue-2/issuetoc

Goldmann, H. (2009, April 8). Achievement Through Technology and Innovation act (ATTAIN) introduced in the Senate. *ISTE Community Ning*, at www.iste-community.org/profiles/blogs/achievement-through-technology

Goldmann, H. (2010, June 28). Ed tech funding chart. In *The future of ed tech in the Obama administration*. A PowerPoint presentation given at the ISTE Annual Conference and Exposition, Denver.

Goldmann, H. (2011, April 12). Ed tech eliminated in final budget bill for FY11. *ISTE Community Ning*. Retrieved from www.iste-community.org/profiles/blogs/ed-tech-eliminated-in-final

International Society for Technology in Education. (2008, June). *Technology and student achievement—The indelible link*. ISTE Policy Brief. Eugene, OR: Author. Retrieved from www.k12hsn.org/files/research/Technology/ISTE_policy_brief_student_achievement.pdf

International Society for Technology in Education. (2008–2009). *Honor, celebrate, envision*. (2008–2009 Annual Report). Eugene, OR: Author. Retrieved from www.iste.org/Libraries/PDFs/ISTE_Annual_Report_2008_2009.sflb.ashx

International Society for Technology in Education. (2009). *ISTE's 2009 U.S. public policy principles and federal & state objectives*. Eugene, OR: Author. Retrieved from www.iste.org/Libraries/PDFs/109_09-US-Public-Policy-Principles.sflb.ashx

International Society for Technology in Education. (2009, June). *ISTE strategic plan*. Eugene, OR: Author. Retrieved June 9, 2010, from www.iste.org/about-iste/governance/strategic-plan.aspx

International Society for Technology in Education (2010). *Exploring excellence*. (2009–2010 Annual Report). Eugene, OR: Author. Retrieved from www.iste.org/Libraries/PDFs/Annual_Report_2010.sflb.ashx

International Society for Technology in Education. (2010). Support $50 million for the preparing teachers for digital age learners act. [Press release.] Eugene, OR: Author.

International Society for Technology in Education. (2010). *Standards for global learning in the digital age*. Eugene, OR: Author. Retrieved from www.iste.org/standards.aspx

International Society for Technology in Education. (2010). *Top ten in '10: ISTE's education technology priorities for 2010*. Eugene, OR: Author. Retrieved from www.iste.org/about-iste/advocacy/top-ten-in-10.aspx

International Society for Technology in Education. (2010, May 7). ESEA reauthorization recommendations. Letter to Tom Harkin, Chairman, and Michael Enzi, Ranking Member, Health, Education, Labor and Pensions Commission, United States Senate.

NetDay. (2003). Millennials: Today's students? PowerPoint presentation. Shown at CoSN's ninth annual D-12 School Networking Conference, Arlington, VA, March 4, 2004.

PR Web. (1997–2009). Press release writing fundamentals. Retrieved from http://service.prweb.com/pr/_assets/downloads/pr_writing_Fundamentals.pdf

PR Web. (n.d.) Writing great online news releases. Retrieved May 6, 2011, from http://service.prweb.com/pr/_assets/downloads/how-to-write-press-releases.pdf

Race to the Top Fund. (2009). Authorized by the *American Recovery and Reinvestment Act of 2009*. Retrieved from www2.ed.gov/programs/racetothetop

Race to the Top Assessment program. (2009). Authorized by the *American Recovery and Reinvestment Act of 2009*. Retrieved from www2.ed.gov/programs/racetothetop-assessment/

Schools, Health & Libraries Broadband (SHLB) Coalition. (2011, February 21). *Connections, capacity, community: Exploring potential benefits of research and education networks for public libraries.* (A study commissioned by the Bill and Melinda Gates Foundation.) Retrieved from www.shlbc.org

Universal Service Administrative Company (USAC). (2010). USAC administers the Universal Service Fund. At www.usac.org

Universal Service Fund (USF). (1934, 1996). At www.usac.org/about/universal-service

U.S. Department of Commerce. (2010, September 27). Secretary Locke announces recovery act investments to expand broadband internet access and spur economic growth. [Press release.] Retrieved October 28, 2010, from www.commerce.gov/news/press-releases/2010/09/27/secretary-locke-announces-recovery-act-investments-expand-broadband-i

U.S. Department of Education. (2010, March). Supporting science, technology, engineering, and mathematics education: Reauthorizing the elementary and secondary education act. In *A Blueprint for Reform: The Reauthorization of the Elementary and Secondary Education Act*, at www2.ed.gov/policy/elsec/leg/blueprint/faq/supporting-stem.pdf

U.S. Department of Education. (2010, March 13). *ESEA reauthorization: A blueprint for reform.* (The Obama administration's blueprint for revising the Elementary and Secondary Education Act.) Retrieved March 15, 2010, from www2.ed.gov/policy/elsec/leg/blueprint/index.html

U.S. Department of Education. (2011). *The federal role in education: Overview.* Retrieved May 3, 2011, from www2.ed.gov/about/overview/fed/role.html

U.S. General Accounting Office (GAO). (2006, February 1). Anti-Deficiency Act (ADA). In *Principles of Federal Appropriations Law*, third edition, vol. II, chapter 6, part C. Retrieved May 3, 2011, from www.gao.gov/htext/d06382sp.html

U.S. House of Representatives Committee on Appropriations. (2011, April 12). Historic spending cuts the centerpiece for final continuing resolution (CR) for fiscal year 2011. Retrieved April 27, 2011, from http://appropriations.house.gov/index.cfm?FuseAction=PressReleases.Detail&PressRelease_id=285

# CD Contents—Forms, Kits, Templates, and More

## ABCs of Advocacy Forms

- Develop a State/Province Advocacy Plan
- Personal Advocacy Checklist
- State/Province Affiliate Organization Checklist

## Advocacy Kits

- Building Administrators Tool Kit
- Community Tool Kit
- Corporate Community Tool Kit
- District Administrators Tool Kit
- Education Associations Tool Kit
- Policy Makers Tool Kit
- School Boards Tool Kit
- Teachers Tool Kit

## Advocacy Templates

- Advocacy Story Template
- Elevator Pitch Template
- Letter to the Editor Tips and Template
- Policy Brief Tips and Template
- Press Release Template
- Stakeholders Tips and Strategies
- Talking Points Model

- Template for Inviting Policy Makers
- Tips for Contacting and Inviting Policy Makers

## and More

- Congressional Scavenger Hunt (Learn more about your legislators)
- *Learning & Leading with Technology* articles:
  - "Become a Better Advocate for Ed Tech"
  - "Raise Your Voice to Win Back Ed Tech Funding!"
- Lobbying Basics (for example, Lobbying vs. Advocacy)
- SIG Advocacy Position Statements:
  - SIGAdmin       SIGMS
- Technology Update Flyer (Example from Alaska to share at meetings)
- Webinar presented by Advocacy and Affiliate Committees of ISTE (Link):
  "Learning How to Make Your Voice Heard"